To Jack Falvey,
One of the best pros
and professional colleagues
I have met.

Sincerely,

Jim Evered
5/7/01

Shirt-Sleeves
Management

Shirt-Sleeves Management

JAMES F. EVERED

amacom

A Division of American Management Associations

Library of Congress Cataloging in Publication Data

Evered, James F
  Shirt-sleeves management.

  Includes index.
  1. Personnel management.   I. Title.
  HF5549.E86   658.3   80-67962
  ISBN 0-8144-5636-7

© 1981 AMACOM
A division of American Management Associations, New York.
All rights reserved. Printed in the United States of America.

First Printing

Acknowledgments

Without the help of many people, this book would never have become a reality. I therefore include three acknowledgments:

To my wonderful bride of twenty-eight years, Joanne, who has tolerated my dedication to my work, who has been my equalizer. She knew how to build my confidence when I needed it; she knew how to kick the pedestal from under me when I needed that. She was, and is, a great manager.

To my son, Erich, a successful manager in his own right, who spent countless hours editing Dad's manuscript to clean up the grammar and sharpen the diction.

To the many managers and supervisors who have, without knowing it, contributed to this book. I have embraced their good qualities and have wholeheartedly condemned their shortcomings. My thanks to all of them.

Contents

Introduction

The manager or supervisor who doesn't need help doesn't exist. Unfortunately, the sources to which a manager turns for help often turn out to be impractical, theoretical, confusing, and complicated. This is true of many books, seminars, packaged programs, customized programs, and audiovisual programs. Often the more sophisticated, theoretical, and complicated a program is, the more marketable it is. It seems to contain more, so you might naturally expect to get more from it. The opposite is often true.

The basic and practical concepts of managing people don't need to be complicated. This book is written for the manager or supervisor who is seeking practical, validated, down-to-earth, and effective means of improving his or her management effectiveness. When the manager is more effective, so is the entire work group. The returns in productivity are in direct proportion to the size of the work group. It doesn't matter whether the group is made up of sales personnel, production personnel, office personnel, hourly labor, or skilled, technical, or highly specialized personnel; the basic concepts of effective management are pretty much universal.

The primary thrust of this book may be somewhat different from others in that most of the emphasis will be on the management of *people.* I am far less concerned with managing the "administrivia" of the job than I am with the supervision of people. Companies succeed only when the people within the organization succeed at their individual jobs. Companies produce nothing; people within companies produce everything, including the profits, earnings, savings, products, and services.

A productive, stable work environment is invariably characterized by the effective management of people. Relationships between supervisors and subordinates will be healthy, morale will be high, and positive attitudes will abound. Conversely, when the relationship is less than ideal, productivity suffers, high employee turnover is common, and the work output never reaches full potential. If it is *people* who make things happen, obviously a disciplined effort to improve the way the people are managed will be reflected right on the bottom line of the operating statement.

The relationship that exists between managers and their employees is a key element in productivity. That relationship is the basis of attitudes that have a direct bearing on output and profitability, the two key elements by which any manager's performance is measured. My primary objective in writing this book is to help you strengthen the relationship between you and your people, to improve the output and profitability of your work group, no matter how small or large that work group may be.

Managing is managing, any way you look at it. The basic concepts of influencing another's behavior are fairly universal, whether you are responsible for a large workforce or a two-man operation. If you are responsible for the activities of another person, you are a manager. Your title may be supervisor, director, foreman, boss, owner, or manager. Your duties are still managing and directing the activities of others.

Owners of retail businesses often feel no need to train personnel or manage them with professional techniques. They feel they're too small. But their employees often form a larger group than many of the work groups within a large corporation. They are no less important. They need managing, training, and motivating every bit as much. Their impact on the retail business may be greater than the impact of one work group on the large corporation. Therefore, training and managing may be even more important to the business owner.

Any manager or supervisor who wants to improve can do so. Do you want to increase the productivity of your work group? Do you want your people to be happier in their work? Do you want them to strive for greater achievement—willingly? Do you want to make your job of managing easier? If so, the concepts presented in this book can help you. Whether you are a newly appointed manager or one with a lot of experience, there is a wealth of information in this book that can help.

Throughout the past two decades I have learned a lot from managers in scores of industries and in more than twenty countries. After you have worked with a large number of managers in a large variety of work situations, you begin to develop what might be called the ideal management profile, as much as such a thing exists. You learn to recognize those management techniques that have a high frequency of success. You also learn to recognize many common management practices that are counterproductive. You are then in a position to accept those that work best, and reject or discourage the ones that may have a negative effect on a work group.

I am averse to presenting concepts that have not been validated. The techniques presented in this book work. They are techniques I have taught successful managers for years. Sure, the content of my management seminars has changed over the years as new concepts are developed and validated. People change, conditions change, and values change. As a result, management styles have had to change. For example, the style of managing the younger worker of today is quite different from styles that worked on young people twenty years ago. Today's young workers are far more educated and independent and far less security conscious than their counterparts of the 1950s and 1960s. They must be managed differently. Many older managers find it difficult to accept this fact of life.

Today, younger people are moving into the workforce in massive numbers. They are moving rapidly up the management ladder, and they are bringing with them a different set of values. These values are not necessarily wrong or right—just different. The new employees must be managed in light of *their* values. Managers who fail to recognize this are wasting an enormous human resource, for these young people readily leave a working environment that fails to tune in to their values.

I know of many successful older managers who have changed with the times and are extracting incredible accomplishments from today's younger workforce. They recognize the potential for what it is, accept their employees as they are, and manage accordingly. The most delightful part of it is that these young workers respond in a very positive manner to supervisors who try to understand them.

I was amused in talking to an older office manager recently about his reactions. He moved into a job and inherited a workforce of younger people. He changed style and began to listen to these people, managing them as he thought they would like to be managed. His conclusion was, "These kids are a lot more fun to manage and work with."

I think there's a message in this for all of us. We should never get so old or so experienced that we lose our flexibility. We must try to understand people as they are, accept them as they are, and manage them in that light. Helping you to understand your people and helping you to manage both your younger and your older employees as they are is what this book is all about.

Approach the book with an open mind. Take it all the way through, and then draw your conclusions. I have tried to bring you the best I have been able to glean from two decades of my own management experience, plus the best of all the managers I have known and with whom I have worked. I have attempted to bring you the concepts that will make your job easier and more enjoyable, and at the same time bring out the best in your employees. These are invaluable objectives.

Why, then, do we find managers who neither want nor accept help? These people constitute one of the roots of management weakness witnessed in so many organizations today. Many managers are simply suffering from an erroneous self-concept. They are incapable of seeing themselves as fallible; they blame their weaknesses, mistakes, and low productivity on others. They find it next to impossible to be objective about themselves, overestimating their importance and feeling that their positions are more important than their responsibilities. They see themselves as being responsible *for* their employees, but have never perceived themselves as being responsible *to* their employees.

This kind of thinking, unfortunately, has a reciprocal effect that tends to compound the problem. The manager who harbors an erroneous self-concept usually has a completely erroneous concept of others. Preoccupied with self-worth, the manager finds it impossible to take a truly objective view of others in the work group. This manager basically mistrusts others, refuses to delegate properly, makes all the decisions, takes all the credit, rationalizes mistakes, and invariably fails to develop the full potential of the members of the work group. The supervisor/subordinate relationship under these circumstances can be very counterproductive.

Such a manager perceives employees as incompetent, and treats and manages them as incompetents. Result? Incompetency. They are seen as lazy and indifferent, and they react to this image. Productivity suffers. They are never allowed to make decisions. Result? Lack of employee growth and development.

By no means does the above represent the majority of managers. Fortunately, most people in management or supervisory positions are constantly looking for ways to improve their effectiveness. But even the manager who, to a degree, suffers either an erroneous self-concept or an erroneous concept of others can learn to identify personal shortcomings and can do something about correcting them. This book can be of enormous help to an individual who is in this situation.

I am aiming primarily at any manager who is concerned with employee growth and development, who is seeking practical and understandable ways of achieving them, and who sees subordinates as capable, educated, adult, normal human beings who want just about the same things out of life the manager wants.

The principles I will present in this book apply to both men and women. Throughout my career, I have found no significant difference between male and female managers in their performance and achievement. The same is true for jobs other than management. However, to avoid monotony, and for purposes of simplification, I shall use he, his, him, and himself in a generic sense. This will make reading easier and will help to avoid the clumsiness of he/she, his/her, and related terms.

As the concepts are presented, a model will be developed to help put the management function into a perspective that makes sense. It will show the relationships between you and your employees that lead to teamwork, cooperation, self-motivation, and greater productivity. It can make your job of managing others a lot easier and more enjoyable and give you the satisfaction of seeing more self-growth among your employees.

As you conclude each chapter you will be able to develop an evaluation of supervisory practices (ESP rating) to determine the extent to which you follow or agree with the concepts presented. It will be a list of questions that will also serve as a brief review of the material presented. Any questions to which you reply with a "no" should cause you to think a little harder about your particular management style. These could well be your targets for a self-development program.

I strongly suggest that you answer each question with a pencil as you proceed through the book. After completing the book, go back through each ESP rating; I'm sure you will then change "no" to "yes" in many cases. The changes will indicate that you have gained additional insight into your relationship with your employees, insight that could have a positive impact on your management style and the productivity of your entire work group. This insight is one of the aims of my book.

1 | The Right Perspective

Your Contractual Arrangement

You have, in essence, a contractual arrangement with each of your subordinates. You have a perfect right to expect certain things from each of them: a full day's work, in-job growth, the meeting of objectives, loyalty, cooperation, honesty, and maximum productivity.

They, too, have a perfect right to expect certain things from you: guidance, support, training, encouragement, trust, faith, and honesty. As with any contract, it is a two-way street where each party has certain obligations to the other. Unless you can establish this concept firmly in your mind, your job as a manager will be much more difficult. If you don't fulfill your part of the bargain, you have no moral right to expect your employees to fulfill theirs. The fact that you are the boss does not give you a unilateral contract. The better you do in meeting your obligations under the contract, the better your employees will do for you.

Essentially, there are three basic things we expect of an employee: *commitment*, *ability*, and the *drive to achieve*.

Commitment. We want an employee to be wholeheartedly committed to his objectives. We want a strong commitment to com-

8

pany policies and procedures, to group productivity, to company products and services, and to the employee's individual responsibilities. This complete commitment develops a sense of ownership on the part of the employee. The goals become his. We want the employee to think in terms of "*my* company, *my* objectives, *my* customers, *my* job, and *my* management." But this kind of commitment can be neither demanded nor bought. It must be earned. Any employee, yourself included, works a lot harder toward achieving objectives when this sense of ownership exists.

Ability. It seems superfluous to say, but an employee must possess certain skills and knowledge before he can be expected to achieve anything. Normally no employee has all the required skills and knowledge when hired, but it is your responsibility to see that they are continually developed throughout his employment. As with any manager, you try to hire people with as much of the required knowledge and as many of the skills as possible, but from that point on it is a matter of continual development. It should be your objective to develop each employee until he has a high degree of skills and knowledge and is able to attain a high level of productivity.

Drive to achieve. Without that inner drive for achievement, no employee will reach maximum productivity, regardless of ability. All the skills and knowledge in the world are worthless unless they are put to use. There is a big difference between what an employee knows how to do and what he actually does. One of the biggest indications of management weakness is employees who don't do what they can do. There is a great difference between "can do" and "will do."

Few management problems would exist if every employee had a strong sense of commitment, a high degree of skills and knowledge, and a strong drive to achieve individual and group objectives. Unfortunately, this situation rarely exists, but it can certainly be developed with some effort on your part.

How are these things developed? By meeting *your* obligations under the contract. If you are to expect commitment, ability, and a drive to achieve, you must do three things in exchange: *deputize, supervise,* and *energize*. These three things actually form the foundation of any manager's job description.

Deputize. As a manager, you should pass on to your employees the necessary responsibility, authority, and accountability they need to do the job. They develop a sense of ownership in the job. Without them, your staff probably won't feel a high degree of commitment.

Proper delegation is one of the hardest things for most managers to do. They are simply unwilling to "cut the cord" and allow an employee a certain amount of free rein in performing his job. An employee must be allowed to make certain decisions, even at the cost of some mistakes. Without mistakes he will never learn. Without experience in decision making he will never feel a sense of ownership and responsibility in the job. Naturally, the newer the employee the less delegation you can give. However, as he grows, so should his responsibility. He should also have fewer limitations imposed on him.

Three types of manager are most unwilling to delegate even minor decisions. First, the insecure manager feels that delegation takes important facets of the job away from him and weakens his position. If the employees can handle the job alone, perhaps the manager isn't needed. Ridiculous thinking, of course, but it does inhibit the delegation process. This manager doesn't realize that he has jeopardized his own chance of advancement by having employees who are incapable of moving into his position. Failure to delegate and develop employee growth is a self-defeating practice for any manager.

Second is the manager who suffers an erroneous concept of others as well as of self. The manager is unable to believe that each employee is an intelligent, adult human being, capable of all the normal thinking processes. If he is right, he had better take a good hard look at his recruiting and hiring procedures. Proper delegation is an indication of a manager's trust and faith in his people. This trust can go a long way toward building teamwork, loyalty, cooperation, and a sense of ownership.

The third type of manager has an overactive ego. He simply gets his jollies out of retaining all the decision making. The manager finds it a great ego boost to have the employees come to him for all the answers. It is a parental syndrome that gives a great amount of self-satisfaction, and it destroys any effort to gain employee commitment.

Effective managers are those who are willing to cut the cord and delegate as much as possible to their employees. Under modern concepts of management, it is generally felt that decision making should be delegated to the lowest level of the organization at which the decisions could be made. This is one of the reasons a participative style of management, or management by objectives, is so successful. The employee gets a part of the action in decision making and knows that the objectives are influenced by his input. The employee's opinions and suggestions are respected. A manager who seeks and honors the input of his employees understands the synergistic effect it has on the work group—"none of us is as smart as all of us."

An employee wants to be responsible for his part of the group productivity, wants to view it as *his* job, *his* input, *his* output, *his* decisions. He wants to feel a sense of responsibility for meeting group objectives, for getting things done. Without this sense of ownership, the job will not get done to the same degree, regardless of the manager's demands.

Accountability is another important facet of delegation. An employee wants, and has a right to expect, to be measured against the standards of the job. He wants to know how he is doing. Employees with a personal commitment to objectives are willing to accept the elements of risk in not achieving objectives. Without commitment, they want no part of the risk. If your employees willingly accept the risks, they will work harder to avoid the negative consequences of failure to achieve. There is a sense of personal pride in having overcome the risk through achievement.

Supervise. Let's get an open-minded perspective on this word. Many managers can see only the authoritative aspects of supervision—that is, overseeing, watching, giving orders, controlling, making decisions, offering criticism. These are all parts of the supervisory function, but it is essential that a manager see a more complete spectrum.

Practically every book written on the subject of management has divided the function into the old basic categories: planning, organizing, supervising, and controlling. It also seems that most emphasis has been placed on the controlling aspect of the job. Naturally, under this philosophy, a manager quickly develops a feeling that he is responsible for everything. Granted, the manager is responsible for organizing the work group, the workload, and the job functions. He is also responsible for the planning and output of the work group. It is very easy for a manager to become so preoccupied with these responsibilities that he overlooks the fact that he is also responsible *to* his employees.

Supervision means control, but it also means giving, in the form of training, coaching, performance feedback, and counseling. Each of these elements will be covered in subsequent chapters. They are essential to supervising others. Without these kinds of help, no employee can be expected to develop a high level of skills and knowledge. Providing supervision in the full sense of the word is the manager's contribution in exchange for high-level skills and knowledge.

Energize. The manager must act as a battery, providing the energy to maintain full-speed productivity. Without the proper spark, nothing happens. All the skills and knowledge in the world are useless unless the employee is motivated. Skills and knowledge can be taught, but motivation must be provided by the manager. You can't *teach* an employee to be motivated, but you can *cause* one to be. A later chapter will be devoted to motivational techniques, but it is essential for a manager to understand at the outset that his motivational efforts must provide the momentum for reaching objectives. He cannot make a once-in-a-while effort, but must feed the electric power constantly.

Important facets of motivating employees include challenging opportunities, constant reinforcement and encouragement, and proper recognition for results achieved. Unless these are provided by the manager, all else is likely to be lost.

Now, let's look at all the elements mentioned as parts of the contractual arrangements between the manager and his employees. These elements make up the management model shown in Figure 1, which gives you an overall perspective on the relationship and responsibilities between you and your people.

Proper deputizing, with all its elements, develops a personal commitment on the part of the employee. Proper supervision will develop the skills and knowledge necessary for top performance. Proper energizing will develop that inner drive for achievement. When all three are developed, goals and objectives will be met. By the same token, a short circuit anywhere in the model will have an adverse effect on productivity. It is your responsibility to see that no short circuits exist. You are the electrician.

You Are Responsible For Your People

Unless you are solely self-employed, you are responsible for the performance of others—perhaps one person, perhaps hundreds. At any rate, you are responsible to your employer for the productivity of the group. You were promoted or hired into a management or supervisory position because your company felt you had the ability to bring out the best in others, to improve their performance, to get them to go that extra mile. You had set a good example of performance in your previous job and had earned the right to move up into a supervisory position. But now, instead of doing all the work, you are managing others who are doing it. As a manager you must recognize the difference. Otherwise, you will continually have problems developing and maintaining a smooth, productive work group.

The transition from "doing" to "managing" can be difficult unless you develop a proper perspective. Doing and managing require a completely different set of skills, and the sooner you learn this the sooner you will begin to grow into a manager capable of

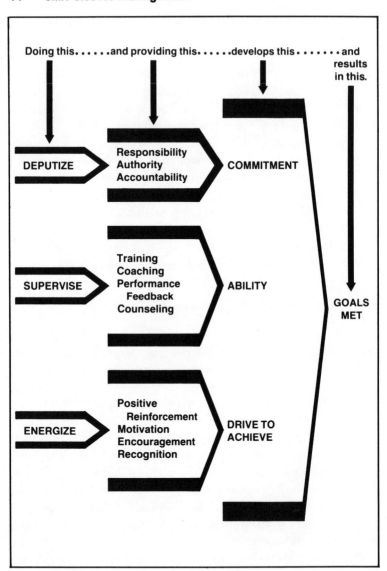

Figure 1. The management model.

bringing out the best in your people. Those who have failed to recognize this difference have never developed into top productive managers.

Your position of leadership cannot—must not—be taken lightly. Your employees' productivity, their future, their contribution to corporate objectives will be in direct proportion to your ability to lead them in productive and profitable channels. Sure, some of the skills you used in the previous job—communicative skills, skills in influencing other people, organizational skills—you will continue to use. But you will also have a new set of skills to master.

Management has often been defined as "getting things done through other people." Unfortunately, the novice manager puts the emphasis on the wrong part of this definition—"through other people." The veteran manager has learned that the emphasis should be on "getting things done." Naturally, you will be working through other people or you wouldn't be a manager. But the productivity you can expect from other people depends entirely on your ability to train and motivate them to high levels of achievement.

Doing a job and getting someone else to do it well are two entirely different skills. You will often find a difference between what an employee should be doing and what that employee is actually doing. In some cases, it will be because of lack of skills or knowledge. If so, it's your job to teach the employee how to do the job. In other cases, the employee simply will not perform the way he was taught. It is then the fault of management, and it is your responsibility to apply the management techniques that will bring the employee back on the right track.

Simply telling an employee to do something right is rarely effective; he must be motivated to do it right. You must analyze why the employee is not performing satisfactorily, so you will know which motivational efforts to apply. To do this right, you need specific management skills.

Every employee working under you is unique. Each has different needs, different skills, different attitudes, different motivational "triggers." You must learn to deal with each as if that employee were the only person in the world. There is no blanket technique for managing that will work on all employees. There is no panacea. There are no pat answers, no style that always works. What works on an employee today may have no effect on him tomorrow. What works on one may have a completely negative effect on another.

Motivating employees is a complex procedure. It requires a thorough understanding of your people: what turns them on at any given point in time, their individual needs, their attitudes toward their job, toward you, and toward the company, and much more. Understanding your staff and applying the proper motivational techniques will determine your "bottom line" contribution to the organization. Knowing people and understanding them are not the same. It is imperative that you develop a high degree of understanding, patience, empathy, and concern for your employees. Otherwise, you may be nothing but a mere figurehead of a manager. It is when you develop a sensitivity to the feelings of your staff that you begin to take command of your job.

Being a manager also has distasteful aspects. At times you will be faced with the need for firm, face-to-face disciplinary actions, for severe criticism, perhaps even for dismissing an employee. You certainly won't find these tasks enjoyable, but they will be necessary. As a manager, you have to face up to disagreeable duties, bite the bullet, and do what you have to do. If you don't have the intestinal fortitude, get out of managing. Otherwise you'll merely be holding down a job someone else should have. If the company is going to pay you to be a manager, the company is entitled to a return on its investment, a return in productivity and effectiveness.

Facing up to management duties can be very difficult for some new managers. This is especially true of the manager who was promoted out of the ranks of the people he must now supervise. He was "one of the boys" for a long time and often finds it difficult to grasp the full spectrum of management tasks and establish his position as supervisor.

I have found this to be particularly true for sales managers. I have seen sales managers fail miserably because they would not take command of the job and manage. They had been part of the gang for too long. They had played golf with other salesmen on Saturdays, visited the local tavern with them, held sales meetings with them, engaged in competitive incentive programs with them, traveled with them, and worked as a team with them for years. Suddenly they are managing instead of selling. They find their new position uncomfortable and even embarrassing. They often find it next to impossible to give orders to their own kind. They stay on the job, hoping the salesman will continue to produce and make them look good. Their stay, however, is often cut short when sales decrease and they are unable or unwilling to step in and take corrective measures. They just don't want to hurt anyone's feelings.

Don't follow this scenario. Accept the full responsibility for the productivity of each member of your work group.

You Are Responsible To Your People

Too few managers understand that they are responsible to their employees as well as for them. As a manager, you have an enormous impact on the lives of your people. In a direct way, you have a bearing on their very life-style, their standard of living, and their future. And your influence on their level of productivity cannot be overemphasized.

You must *mean* something to your employees. It is you to whom they must turn for guidance, for encouragement, for information, for an example, for understanding and strength. Never overlook the importance of their opinion of you as a manager. Their opinion is much more important than your opinion of yourself as a manager. The way they perceive you as a manager will determine how well they will produce for you and for the company. It is imperative that your employees perceive you as a leader, not as a boss.

None of the foregoing implies an abdication of your management responsibilities. There will be times when you must be extremely firm, perhaps dictatorial or demanding. When, of course, depends on circumstances. But when it comes time to be firm, be firm! Stand your ground; make clear-cut decisions; establish your position as a manager and let that position be known. However, you should not be authoritarian except when absolutely necessary.

Most of the time you will be more effective if you show the gentleness of a lamb, put an arm on the shoulder, give a few words of positive encouragement or a pat on the back, or just sit and listen to an employee get his troubles off his chest. We all need words of encouragement, a feeling that we are worthwhile, that we are contributing to something important, that we are respected and recognized. Every individual needs positive reinforcement. It is your responsibility as a manager to see that your employees get it regularly, as a matter of course.

See Your Employees As They Really Are

Every individual, including yourself, wants to be considered a valuable, accepted, contributing, important, adult, educated human being. If you are one of those rare people who can see everyone else in this light, you are well on your way to being a successful professional manager.

We all need a favorable self-image and constant reaffirmation of our worth. As a manager, it is your moral responsibility to see that each of your employees develops a favorable view of himself. The self-image, like every living thing, must be nourished constantly or it will die. A person's self-image may be his most important asset. A favorable self-image builds confidence and self-assuredness. Enthusiasm is an important by-product.

The image a person has of himself is a direct result of that person's background. We are all molded by our experiences. The human mind, just like a computer, absorbs and retains every experience it has ever had. Recorded in your memory bank is everything you have ever read, heard, touched, seen, smelled, tasted, or sensed. It's all there, although admittedly you can only retrieve a minute portion of it.

Just like a computer, you are the product of your own individual programming. No other person in the world is programmed exactly like you. Inputs with the greatest impact on you include those of your parents, teachers, minister, education, experiences, and peers. Your programming began the day you were born. Every experience adds to it, including the material you are reading right now. And the process will continue until the day you die. As a result of your programming inputs, you have a unique set of outputs—certain likes, dislikes, prejudices, fears, biases, attitudes, values, perceptions, goals, and ambitions. Your self-image is also a direct result of your programming.

From a management standpoint, you must recognize that your employees are the products of their programming, not yours. They, too, have unique sets of likes, dislikes, prejudices, and so on. They didn't live your life, so don't expect them to be like you. Accept them as they are, not as you are. Every one of them is unique, with a totally different style of programming. Accept them as they are and manage them as individuals.

Your actions as a manager will continue to program your employees. You will add to their experiences. Be certain they are favorable experiences. You will provide inputs. Be certain they are favorable and productive inputs. Remember, just as with a computer, "garbage in, garbage out." Unless your inputs are favorable and positive, you cannot expect favorable and positive outputs. You have no right to expect them.

Don't try to change an employee's personality. There is no way your inputs can overwhelm the inputs that have made the person what he is. They have been imbedded too deeply for too many years. It would be a difficult chore for a trained psychologist, so for you as a layman it isn't worth trying. The point is this: Don't try to rebuild an employee. Take what you have, accept it as it is, and continue to build on the present structure. What you build will be far more important than anything you could ever repair. You can't make a silk purse out of a sow's ear—unless you start with a silk sow. If you demand certain personality characteristics, find them at the interview table.

Being responsible to your people includes providing motivation. To do this effectively you must learn to read your people so you can identify their motivational triggers. From a programming standpoint, you must learn how each employee's card has been punched. Remember, you can't turn them on until you tune them in. Learning to read employees will be covered in a later chapter.

Your willingness or ability to understand your employees could easily be clouded by your attitude toward managing. That is, your preference for a particular management style is usually affected by your attitudes toward your people. If you feel that your employees are capable, adult, contributing people, you will probably manage by giving them a comparatively free rein and placing considerable reliance on their input and suggestions. If you perceive your people as lazy, incompetent, or indifferent, you will probably embrace a more authoritarian style of management.

Management Style Affects Productivity

Management styles cover the full spectrum from the completely dictatorial and authoritarian to the absolute opposite. Very few managers are found at either extreme, fortunately. The managers in the middle of the spectrum can, perhaps, be defined as participative managers; that is, they maintain a balance between manager control and employee control of the job.

The erroneous self-concept mentioned in the introduction to this book appears at both ends of the spectrum. The manager who adopts a free-rein style usually does so because he underrates his own strengths, lacks self-confidence, and feels uncomfortable in his position. He tends to let the organization run itself. The completely autocratic or authoritarian manager, on the other hand, tends to overrate his own strengths and sees himself as the only person capable of making decisions.

The authoritarian manager is a fascinating man to study and a very frustrating man to work for. It is difficult to understand this man's motives without feeling a deep sense of pity for him. He is often wrought with fear, guilt, and insecurity as a result of past failures. His authoritarianism is a mask—a defense. He must prove to the world that he is successful. As a result of his past he fears failure; therefore, he refuses to gamble on anything, including an attitude of trust toward others. He often views the productivity of others as a threat to his own position. He simply must succeed, even at the expense of others.

This man is out to get everything he can. Giving is not even in his vocabulary. He must exploit to protect his own position. The underlying philosophy of his every move is, "What's in it for me?" His employees are seen as pawns on a chessboard, to be manipulated, even sacrificed if necessary to reach the objective of winning. To him, winning isn't the most important thing, it's the *only* thing; and he perceives the victory as his and his alone.

The authoritarian manager feels that he holds a unilateral contract with his employees. They are to give—he is to receive. He doesn't want participation; he wants obedience. He prefers to surround himself with competent people, for protective reasons, but destroys their initiative through suppressive treatment. He keeps them insecure about their jobs, keeps them on edge, and then wonders why they lose their will to win or to achieve. The manager is their biggest barrier to succeeding.

This management style is the most difficult to change. The manager's insecurity clouds his objectivity. He builds a wall of threats around himself that cannot be permeated by suggestions, advice, love, or opinions. His judgment alone is supreme. Nor will he attempt to get through the wall with respect, trust, confidence, admiration, or generosity. He keeps himself in and others out, all the while maintaining a tight hold on all the puppet strings leading to his people. He is a manipulator who stifles employee productivity, initiative, ambition, and professional development. He destroys the very things that would provide the security he so desperately needs. He is truly his own worst enemy and is certainly bent on self-destruction.

Is there any salvation for the autocratic manager? Of course there is. At this point you may even wonder whether you harbor any autocratic tendencies. If, during the reading of the last few paragraphs, you felt any hostility, there's a strong possibility that you have some authoritarian characteristics that may prove counterproductive to your own personal objectives. If you are at least willing to take an objective look at your style of managing you have taken the first step toward improvement.

At this point I am going to assume that you feel a bit of hostility, that you feel you may have some autocratic tendencies. Therefore, I am going to address the analysis to you.

The first question to ask yourself is why you are autocratic in managing or supervising others. Do you see this as the only style that works for other successful managers? Do you see it as the only style you can trust? Probably not, but you may well be unwilling or at least reluctant to try another style. That's a perfectly natural attitude for somebody with autocratic tendencies. It's one of his characteristics.

Now think through your past, all the way back to and including childhood. Where were your failures? What experiences did you have that you felt were less than successful? What experiences made you worry or feel ashamed? What failures in others particularly impressed you? What may have contributed to any feelings of insecurity you now feel? Regardless of our personal management style, the above questions are appropriate for every last one of us. We can all recall failures, even disasters. We can all recall disasters that have befallen others and hoped they would never happen to us.

But ask yourself honestly whether these failures were really monumental enough to have a significant impact on you today. Probably not. Can they be undone? Definitely not. Don't try to manage today in order to compensate for the past. Shake off the past and forget it, because you can't change it. Just remember, improvement cannot be retroactive. All you have left to work with is the future, so try to look at that future objectively in terms of what you really want out of life and how you can enjoy life with other people.

From a management standpoint, the most important thing you can have going for you is the relationship between you and others, including subordinates, peers, and superiors. I am not necessarily speaking about a "buddy-buddy" relationship. I mean a healthy relationship of trust, respect, and sensitivity, the building blocks of productivity.

Try to see yourself objectively. You probably have more strengths than you realize. With your experience, education, capability, skills, knowledge, and basic intelligence, there is very little justification for any feelings of insecurity. Be proud of your accomplishments, your abilities, and your present status in life.

But be aware of your limitations too. None of us is perfect; don't try to be. There will always be skills to master, knowledge to be absorbed, and attitudes to be changed. See your limitations objectively. They are not so great, but they shouldn't be buried. We all have them. These should become your targets for self-development.

The next step toward improvement is an objective view of others. Remember, I said objective. Be open-minded toward your people and try to see them as they really are. Don't let prejudice, bias, or distrust distort your evaluation. Try to lay aside any previous opinions or judgments and see your people through a new pair of glasses.

What are their strengths? What are their capabilities? What contribution are they making? What could they contribute? What fresh ideas might they bring to the job? How do their educations contribute? What positive personality characteristics do they display?

If you would view each employee objectively and jot down the answers to these questions for each, you would find that you are managing a pretty normal, productive group of people. They have many strengths. They can make significant contributions to your group output. If you can lay aside subjective opinions you'll probably see that they form a normal and valuable group of employees.

Next, take a look at the attitudes your people have toward you, their manager. It's tough to be objective at this point, but it must be done. How do they feel about your relationship with them? Do they have any feelings of fear, insecurity, distrust, anxiety, resentment, disloyalty, or indifference? If so, what are the roots for such feelings? Feelings and attitudes are caused: they don't just happen. Autocratic management styles generate negative attitudes.

Your management style will have a profound effect on productivity, employee complaints, union problems, employee turnover, operational costs, waste, and absenteeism. Several times I have referred to the manager who suffers an erroneous self-concept and an erroneous concept of others. Although erroneous concepts come in varying degrees, they are much more prevalent than you may think. I can illustrate this point by explaining an exercise I have used in management seminars hundreds of times during the past twenty years.

Prior to any discussion regarding erroneous concepts or self-image, I ask each participant to write down three adjectives describing *himself* as a manager. These are collected and laid aside for later use. I then ask the participants to write three adjectives that describe their typical subordinate. These, too, are collected and laid aside.

Following the discussion on erroneous concepts and self-image, I go through each stack of replies, reading them aloud. Without fail, the managers use positive adjectives to describe themselves 100 percent of the time. Their self-evaluations parallel the twelve adjectives in the scout law: trustworthy, loyal, helpful, friendly, and so on. They use such glowing terms as motivated, dedicated, intelligent, mature, and decisive. Not one time in two decades have I seen a single manager describe himself as autocratic, dictatorial, insensitive, or subjective.

But their descriptions of subordinates are a completely different story. The stack will never be 100 percent negative. However, several managers will put down three negative adjectives. There is invariably a significant negative trend in the replies, including such descriptions as lazy, indifferent, demanding, incompetent, ignorant, careless, irresponsible, and abrasive. Now think about it! Are we so good, and our subordinates so bad? I think not. Managers are simply unable to view either themselves or others objectively.

Basically, the problem relates to self-image. A good one is the most important asset a person has. We will do anything to protect or enhance our self-image, especially if we suffer insecurities. If you would like to see this phenomenon in action, just sit quietly and listen the next time you are with a group of people. Notice how often something is said for the sole purpose of enhancing the speaker's image. We talk about our successes, our achievements, how we outsmarted someone, how dedicated we are to work so hard and suffer so miserably for our company, we drop names, we talk about books we have read and places we have been. Why? To enhance the image we try to project to others.

When managers write down adjectives to describe themselves, they are projecting the image they want others to have of them. They have shortcomings, but they don't want the world to know about them. We just don't want others to see our weaknesses, because that would constitute a threat to our self-image.

I am going to describe an incident that illustrates the defense mechanism a person will employ when the self-image is threatened. I certainly don't recommend that you try this, but I will do something like this at times for the sole purpose of observing the self-image being protected.

I was sitting in the office of a colleague in the training profession. It was my first visit to his company. On his bookshelf I noticed a full set of Shakespearean volumes. It was obvious that he was attempting to project an intellectual image to others. I was quite certain, having known him for four years, that he was no fan of Shakespeare. Without saying a word, I reached toward the bookshelf and pulled out one volume. The book cracked loudly as I opened it, making it quite obvious that it had never been opened. I had challenged his image.

The instant the book cracked, he smiled and said, "I just got them." I immediately thumbed to the front of the volume and said with surprise, "A 1949 copyright?" His image had been threatened again and I knew he would do something to protect it—and he did. He immediately confessed (?), "The truth is, they belong to my wife. She likes to read that kind of stuff." I thought I had gone far enough so I let the issue die right there. I didn't have the heart to ask why she didn't keep the books at home.

Why do we drive cars that are far more expensive than we really need? It projects an image of success to others. We want the world to see us as successful, so we surround ourselves with things that enhance that image. Few women wear a mink coat for the sole purpose of keeping warm. No, they want to be seen as successful. It's just human nature. And adorning themselves with expensive jewelry is certainly not limited to women. Notice how often a man is seen wearing a ring with a diamond that looks as if it could stop up the kitchen sink. It projects an image of success. If you were to challenge that image, that man would probably tell you, "It's a good investment, the way diamonds are going up." You could probably make a safe bet that he will never sell it. Investment? No, it's self-image.

When someone threatens the image we wish to project, we feel angry, hostile, or frustrated, and almost immediately we employ some type of defense to restore that image. But it is not only others who threaten our self-image. The image can be threatened by our own actions or by circumstances. When that happens we feel embarrassed or ashamed. Think of how embarrassed you felt when visitors came to see you as you were lying flat on your back in the hospital in that ridiculous open gown.

No man likes to be seen in such a weakened situation. It destroys the "macho" image he would rather project. Why are men so reluctant to vent their emotions with a good cry? Catch a man with tears in his eyes as he is watching a touching scene on television and he will swear he has something in his eye. Challenge the fact that he drives a $15,000 automobile and he will swear he has back trouble and that it was the only comfortable car he could find.

A favorable self-image is important to all of us. We need to feel good about ourselves, to see ourselves as capable, adult, successful, well-liked human beings. Yes, your self-image is very important to you. It is probably the most important asset you have.

But let's remember one thing. Every last one of your employees is in the same boat. Their self-images are as important to them as yours is to you. It is extremely important that your people develop a positive, favorable self-image, and you should do everything possible to help them develop it. Each night before going to bed, you should ask yourself, "What have I done today to make every one of my people think better of himself? What have I done to improve his or her self-image?"

Sensitivity toward another person's feelings and self-image is the reason we criticize an employee in private. It saves face. No one likes to be told that his performance is unsatisfactory, or that he has made mistakes. That is a threat to his image of success. However, far less damage is done when the criticism is delivered in a sensitive way—in private.

One of the chief marks of a professional manager is a strong sensitivity toward the feelings of others. He does everything possible to help his people develop favorable feelings toward themselves. At the same time he avoids situations that would cause undue damage. He criticizes and corrects, but in a sensitive manner.

Evaluation of Supervisory Practices (ESP Rating)

1. Do my employees feel a sense of ownership in and commitment to individual and group objectives?
2. Am I willing to "cut the cord" and delegate as much as I can?
3. Do I feel that I can delegate without weakening my position as manager?
4. Do I solicit input from my employees in making significant decisions?
5. Do I honestly feel a sense of responsibility *to* my employees, as well as *for* them?
6. Am I willing to face up to the distasteful parts of managing when the situation warrants it?

7. Do my employees perceive me as a leader rather than a boss?

8. Do I perceive each of my subordinates as an adult, educated, sensitive, valuable, and contributing human being?

9. Do I accept each employee as he is and manage him accordingly, rather than try to manage everyone the same way?

10. Am I willing to be objective about my own limitations?

11. Am I willing to be objective about the strengths of my people?

12. Do I make a concerted effort to help my people develop more favorable images of themselves?

2 | Recruiting and Selecting Employees

Planning Ahead

As a manager, you will look only as good as your employees make you look. Your productivity will be the sum of their productivities. Your bottom-line contribution will be the sum of their bottom-line contributions. For purely selfish reasons, you cannot afford any compromises in the selection of your people. The best way to avoid compromising is to plan well ahead.

Naturally, sudden situations may occur that will leave you little time for selection, but the hazard can be minimized by careful planning. Don't get caught so that you have to "manage by crisis." You can build a file of potential employees from which to draw when necessary. The fact that these people may be working somewhere else makes no difference. If your job opportunities are attractive enough, you can get them anyway. Don't think you have to draw your staff from the ranks of the unemployed.

Job Specs Versus People Specs

Maximum productivity comes only when the right people are matched with the right jobs. This may sound like a moot point, but personnel surveys indicate that the majority of American

29

workers dislike what they do for a living. Some of these people are stuck in their jobs because they simply can't do anything else. Some don't have the intestinal fortitude to make a change. But many are unhappy because they are mismatched; they are not in a job that utilizes their particular skills and potential.

Many people accept lesser jobs at the entry level in order to get into a certain company, with aspirations of moving into more challenging jobs in the future. But all too often, supervisors fail to recognize or utilize the employee's capabilities, and the employee is kept at the lower level of productivity until the job becomes routine and boring. The employee may then quit his job and look for a challenging opportunity with another company. This is an unfortunate waste of human resources.

It is not unusual to find highly capable secretaries, for example, working in a typing pool where a very minimum of their potential is being utilized, potential that includes stenography, organizational skills, analytical skills, verbal skills, and the ability to work well with people. In a very real sense, these capable people are underemployed. Both the employee and the employer are suffering from this waste.

Granted, managers often hire at the entry level until a more responsible position opens into which the employee can move. There's nothing wrong with this, as long as a reasonable opportunity is anticipated. Promotions cannot be promised, but a real opportunity must be present. Otherwise, valuable employees will be lost through boredom and discouragement, and the manager will be right back at the starting gate again.

If you want to have a team of properly matched employees, you must have a firm grasp on the specifications for the job so they match the specifications demanded in your recruiting efforts. Obvious? Don't kid yourself! You would be surprised at how often a manager's perception of required job skills is inaccurate. Too many managers fly by the seat of the pants and really can't identify the specific skills required. Their perceptions are often tainted by their biases, prejudices, opinions, and poor observation.

Then, too, many managers don't know how to determine whether an applicant has the skills to match the job. Almost everyone has a gut feeling that he knows exactly what the specs are, and has a great "feel" for selecting candidates. This is a myopic view, unless you happen to be a professional in personnel or employee relations. Be absolutely certain of the job specs and of how to determine people specs. This is the only sure way. Take the time to study both and avoid compromising the productivity of the work group.

Identify the Specific Skills and Knowledge

What must an employee do and what must the employee know in order to perform satisfactorily? The best starting point is the written job description. If you don't have a written job description, write one or get one written. A subsequent chapter will help you develop one. Any manager who doesn't have a current written job description for each member of the work group is already flying by the seat of the pants. If you are one of those people who think job descriptions are unnecessary, you are making your job of managing that much more difficult.

In determining the skills and knowledge required, there are two essential sources—the written job description and on-the-job observation as the work is being done. Above all, make a written list of the specifications, and limit the list to those required.

Skills are observable, measurable behavior. For example:

Operate a fork lift properly and safely
Read and interpret blueprints
Operate an air hammer
Drive a truck properly
Speak Spanish with relative fluency
Write grammatically correct technical reports
Calculate gross profit margins
Rough wire a frame home

Install all bathroom fixtures per code requirements
Communicate clearly and distinctly
Post accounts payable and receivable properly
Use a slide rule properly
Paint and trim cabinets
Type 65 words per minute and take dictation at 150 words per
    minute
Fly a single-engine airplane by instrument
Lift weights of up to 125 pounds safely

These are all observable behaviors.

Only after you have listed the skills required are you in a position to find a candidate to match those skills. Again, it is important to write a list of the skills for each job within the work group. Just for practice, choose any job within your work group, and write a list of the required skills for that job. Next, turn to the job description for that job to see if you have omitted any essential skills. Then observe an employee doing that job. You will probably find you have omitted important tasks. A complete list of requirements should become the base from which you develop your people specifications.

There is also a certain basic knowledge a person must have in order to perform properly. Some of it is difficult to differentiate from skills, but that is unimportant. Again, turn to the job description and to on-the-job observation to develop a list of required knowledge. For example, it is obvious that a person must have a knowledge of the Spanish language if he is to speak it. A person must know some mathematics if he is to compute gross profit margins. Don't worry about skills overlapping. Just go ahead and start a list of what the employee must know. Following are some examples:

Knowledge of basic arithmetic, including addition, subtraction,
    multiplication, and long division
Technical vocabulary, particularly in geology
Familiarity with federal building codes

Knowledge of pigment-mixing combinations
Basic knowledge of human anatomy
Knowledge of basic accounting procedures
Knowledge of hydraulics
Knowledge of provisions of Title VII of the Civil Rights Act
Knowledge of state driving regulations
Familiarity with safe handling procedures for hazardous liquids

After you have completed your list of the skills and knowledge required on the job, it would be well to prepare a specification sheet for each job in the work group, similar to the specification sheet shown in Figure 2. This sheet will be invaluable as you seek candidates for a specific job. Your files should have at all times a current specification sheet for every position in your work group. This will help avoid crises when selecting personnel.

As you develop the specification list, avoid packing it with such nebulous statements as understands the importance of good customer relations, able to get along with others, appreciates quality products, trustworthy, loyal, helpful, friendly, courteous, kind, obedient, cheerful, thrifty, brave, clean, and reverent. These are all excellent qualities, but don't clutter your list with qualities you can't observe or measure. They do nothing but confuse the employee selection procedure. Stick to the job and its specific requirements.

It is highly doubtful that you will be able to find someone who meets all the requirements, but you certainly want someone who meets most or many of them. Any deficiencies in skills or knowledge will become your targets for training after hiring. Chapter 6 is devoted to training.

Sources for Candidates

Wherever there are people, there are candidates, and there are many ways of reaching them. But remember, dig your well before you're thirsty. Avoid panic hiring whenever possible. Begin *now* to build your file of potential employees.

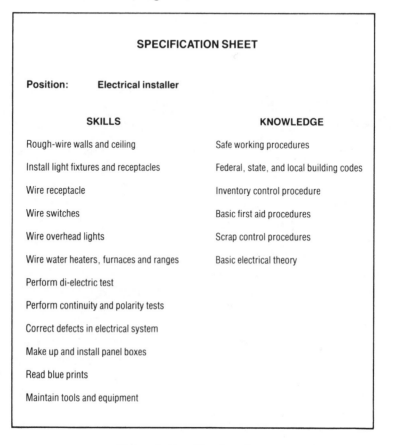

SPECIFICATION SHEET

Position: **Electrical installer**

SKILLS	KNOWLEDGE
Rough-wire walls and ceiling	Safe working procedures
Install light fixtures and receptacles	Federal, state, and local building codes
Wire receptacle	Inventory control procedure
Wire switches	Basic first aid procedures
Wire overhead lights	Scrap control procedures
Wire water heaters, furnaces and ranges	Basic electrical theory
Perform di-electric test	
Perform continuity and polarity tests	
Correct defects in electrical system	
Make up and install panel boxes	
Read blue prints	
Maintain tools and equipment	

Figure 2. Specification sheet.

Avoid the familiar trap of relying on competitors for your job candidates. They have always looked like the ideal source because their employees already have experience and you may not need to train them. This industrial incest has weakened many organizations and has made a substantial contribution to high employee turnover.

Then, too, the practice raises several valid questions. If the employee is any good, why is he available? If the employee left one company, will he leave this one at the next job offer? Is the employee stable? Does he have any company loyalty? Is your job so attractive that another competitor couldn't possibly offer something better? Does the employee still have a personal pipeline back to your competitor? All these questions raise serious doubts about the wisdom of competitors as a source of candidates. Sure, experience is valuable, but it may be well to look for candidates who gained their experience with similar industries or companies rather than with direct competitors.

Your personal day-to-day contacts, such as civic organizations, church groups, Parent-Teachers Association, bowling team, friends, and neighbors, are the best places to begin. Talk to people about the job opportunities you offer from time to time. Ask them to refer any good candidates to you. Your present employees may know of some highly qualified people who would like to be on your work team. Your employees are excellent ambassadors of your company. They know what benefits a job offers. They know the job requirements. They know the type of candidate who would make a meaningful contribution to their team effort. Get acquainted with the people at employment agencies and the state or federal employment office. Let them know the kind of people you need from time to time. They can refer many good candidates.

You probably won't turn to employment advertising until you have an opening, but if you have planned ahead and built a file of candidates, you may not need to advertise. However, if advertising becomes necessary, there are a few rules that could save you a lot of time at the interview table. They may help you avoid spending your time with unemployed drifters or people looking for a temporary job until they find what they want.

Read the employment ads in your local newspaper first. Study those ads that have the greatest appeal for you. What is the style, format, wording, layout, and so on? How much information do they present? What is the most attractive feature of each? Do they define the job in specific terms? Would they weed out "lookers" or drifters? Pay particular attention to the ads placed by the employment agencies. These agencies are professionals and you can learn a lot from them.

When you are ready to write your ad, try some of the ideas listed below. These are suggested guidelines for writing an advertisement. Not all items will necessarily be appropriate for every ad.

1. Define the job in specific terms—electrician for rough wiring of new homes, retail salesperson to sell sporting goods, journeyman plumber, cabinet builder, secretary, offset press operator, night watchman for lumberyard.

2. Include any technical requirements (but be certain they are actually needed)—degree in electrical engineering, geological engineer with petroleum background, licensed electrician, degree in basic accounting, minimum two years' study in corporate law.

3. Include salary offered—$15,000 to start, $4.50/hour, salary range 20–25K, straight commission plus bonus.

4. If established, include hours and days of work—8–5 Monday to Friday.

5. Don't itemize company benefits. Everyone today has approximately the same plan. It is enough to say "excellent benefits" or "competitive benefits." If the applicant's main concern is benefits, you may not want to hire him.

6. State that you are an equal opportunity employer. Under today's federal regulations, you had better be one, too.

7. If appropriate, state time and dates to apply, whether résumés are to be sent in, whether to apply in person, telephone contact only. Naturally, state whom and where to contact, including address and/or phone number.

8. Write your ad first. Then see how much space you must buy to get it printed. Don't try to cut an ad down to fit a cheap space. Make sure your ad is an investment, not an expense. A good ad is worth paying for. Take the time and space to do it right.

9. If you want your ad to stand above the roar of the others, be innovative, be different. You may wish to run your ad in solid reverse (white print on a solid black background). The newspaper can offer various borders to highlight your ad. Innovation will maximize attention, impact, and impression.

View your ad as if *you* were a potential candidate. What would you want to know before you took the time to apply? What would make the job attractive to you? Does it seem suited to your particular talents and interests? Does it seem more attractive than your present job?

Keep Everything Legal

Unless you can afford to face a suit for discrimination, you had better brush up on the latest legal technicalities in hiring. The laws with which you are most concerned are the Civil Rights Act of 1964, including Title VII; the Age Discrimination in Employment Act; the Fair Labor Standards Act; the Equal Employment Opportunity Act of 1972; the Equal Pay Act of 1963; and some executive orders that have been issued. There are several other laws of equal importance that you must consider to be certain you stay within legal guidelines in your interviewing, hiring, promotion, termination, and opportunity practices.

It would be both impossible and impractical to include all the information here that relates to these legal pitfalls. I suggest you write to the Research Institute of America, 589 Fifth Avenue, New York, New York 10017, ordering a copy of its latest published "Guidelines on Preemployment Screening." The small investment may save you from a lot of legal entanglements.

The institute's guidelines cover, in understandable form, what you can and cannot do, can and cannot ask during interviews, and can and cannot have on an application form, how to gather background information, how you may use that information, and the regulations covering hiring, promoting, and terminating employees. In other words, it is a special report on staying out of trouble, and as such is worth its weight in gold. It is not the only source of information regarding legalities, but you'll find it one of the most helpful and practical, written in condensed shirt-sleeve English.

In hiring and handling employees, you must lay aside any preconceived notions, biases, and prejudices, like it or not. You no longer have the option of being prejudiced regarding race, color, creed, religion, handicaps, age, or sex. Such prejudice is a thing of the past and you might as well face up to it. There was never any validity in it anyway.

The Interview

The interview gives you an opportunity to determine whether the applicant meets the specifications of the job. Try to ignore gut feelings. Base your hiring decision on valid data. Just remember, you are hiring talent, not selling jobs, so listen more than you talk. Sure, you may be desperate to fill a vacancy, but don't let the urgency cloud your better judgment. A mismatch could be a costly mistake.

Proper interviewing requires time, so plan to take long enough to do it right. Allot a period without interruptions. Stop the phone calls, hang up a "do not disturb" sign, and close the door. Allow nothing short of death, injury, or fire to disturb the interview. An interruption will invariably come just as an applicant has finally begun to open up and tell you the things you really need to know. In-depth probing can be completely destroyed by interruptions. Don't allow them.

Here are some helpful rules for conducting a meaningful and productive interview:

Lay aside enough uninterrupted time.
Be sure the room is comfortable for both you and the applicant.
Make the applicant do most of the talking; guide him with pertinent questions.
Don't ask any questions if the answer is already on the applica-

tion form. (It doesn't make you look particularly brilliant when the information is right there in front of you.)

Always begin by putting the applicant at ease with a few small-talk remarks. Remember, all applicants are a little nervous.

Take notes during the interview. Don't rely on memory when you are interviewing several applicants.

Keep the interview friendly and comfortable all the way. Avoid Gestapo interrogation techniques.

Listen carefully to everything the applicant says.

Try to get a feeling for the applicant's opinions, attitudes, mood, and feelings.

Make encouraging sounds, like "yes," "I see," and "uh-huh," to keep the applicant talking.

Don't be afraid to ask personal or difficult questions. Probe until you get the information you need. Check your legal guidelines concerning questions you may or may not ask. Certain questions could lead to an unintentional violation of civil rights. The difficulty lies not so much in what you ask, but in how you *use* the information as you reach a hiring decision.

Compliment the applicant on any information that is favorable.

If you are turning the applicant down, relay that information tactfully. Don't leave an applicant hanging and wondering unnecessarily.

If you have several applicants to see, and you certainly should, let each know exactly when he may expect to hear from you, and do get in touch and let him know what decision you have reached.

Never help a candidate by suggesting the correct answer. An example: "You aren't afraid of hard work, are you?" Only an idiot would say yes to that one.

If the applicant gives a vague answer, keep probing with questions until you have the details you want.

Remember your objective: to see whether the applicant has the *people specs* to match the *job specs*. A host of questions must be asked if you are to gain objective data on which to base your hiring decision.

Applicants are usually somewhat apprehensive, often defensive. They want the job or they wouldn't be applying. They have the normal fear that they won't make a good impression and won't get the job. They fear rejection. They are often afraid you will learn something about them that will cause you to reject them. As a result, they become defensive and divulge no more information than necessary. They volunteer no information and answer only the questions you pose. Use every interviewing skill available to gather enough data for an objective hiring decision. It is the professional way to build a productive work group.

Under today's hiring legalities, it is well to review some basic standards before you go into an interview. It is essential that you be realistic in matching people specs to job specs, all within legal limitations. These standards should be reviewed, reflected on, and incorporated into your understanding.

Age. An applicant who possesses the physical health and ability to perform well in the job is acceptable, regardless of age. The legal age for minors is significant, but you can no longer reject, for example, a fifty-year-old applicant because you want "a younger employee who will be with us longer." That is clearly age discrimination, which can result in a civil rights suit.

Sex. A person who has the physical strength, stamina, and general physical condition to perform well in the job is acceptable as an applicant, regardless of sex.

Education. A person who has the verbal skills, general intelligence, and social skills that match the established duties and responsibilities of the job is deemed to satisfy the educational requirements. A requirement of "high school diploma only" or "college graduates only" may be extremely difficult to defend in a courtroom; you must be able to prove its relevance to the job under consideration.

Appearance. Within reason, the appearance of an applicant is a surface feature and secondary to ability, credentials, and motivation.

Application form. Inability to complete your company's application form neatly and accurately may be indicative of a lack of communications skills and/or motivation on the applicant's part. However, don't be picky about a couple of misspelled words unless proper grammar and spelling are essential ingredients of the job. They could simply be the result of an applicant's nervousness at the moment.

Within legal bounds, you have a perfect right to use probing questions to learn as much as possible about the applicant. Your decision will have a direct bearing on both your future and the applicant's future, so leave no stone unturned.

What you need to learn, of course, depends on the job in question, but several items are fairly generic to most jobs:

Did the applicant grow up in a working environment?
What is his reaction to authority or criticism?
Is he willing to accept challenging responsibilities?
Does he have a history of achievement and ambition?
Is he willing to learn and grow?
Does he have relevant experience?
Does he seem to display healthy attitudes toward supervision, lines of authority, and communication?
Does he have the required physical, mental, and social ability?
Does he have the ability to manage his finances within the proposed salary?
Does he seem to have self-discipline?
Is he stable?

Keeping the interview organized will help avoid overlooking needed information. Take it step by step through a logical sequence of periods in the applicant's life: early life, high school years, college years, military service, work experience, specific interests, overall attitudes, and communication skills.

Early life. Here is where you learn whether the applicant grew up in a working environment, has accepted work as a way of life, and expects rewards in proportion to energy expended. Open up the questioning regarding the applicant's early life with a broad question, such as, "Could you tell me something about your childhood, your family, where you grew up, and what it was like?" After you have opened up the area of questioning, probe deeper or further:

"What type of work did your father do?"
"Did your mother work?"
"At what age did you have your first job? What was it?"
"What did you like about your first job? What did you dislike?"
"What are some early life experiences you particularly remember?"
"Tell me about your brothers and sisters."

High school years. Again, use a broad question to open the topic: "Now, tell me about your years in high school." Then probe deeper. Of course, if the applicant is a college graduate with twenty years of work experience, his high school experiences could be irrelevant by now.

"What were your favorite subjects? Why?"
"What subjects did you dislike? Why?"
"Describe three of your favorite teachers."
"Why were they your favorites?"
"Tell me about your high school principal."
"Tell me about your jobs during high school."
"What problems did you face as a teenager?"
"What did you like most about being a teenager?"

College years. Start with a broad question: "Can you tell me something about the years you spent in college?" Then continue to probe:

"What were your favorite subjects, professors, instructors? Why?"
"What jobs did you hold, including part-time jobs?"
"Tell me about your supervisors."

"Why did you choose that particular course of study?"
"How, exactly, did you plan to utilize your education?"
"If you could do it all over, how would you do it differently?"
"How did you finance your college education?"
"Why didn't you go farther in your schooling?"

Military experience (if applicable). "I see you were in the service for three years. Tell me about it."

"What about your specific assignments and locations?"
"What did you like most? Dislike?"
"Tell me about your superiors."
"What about special courses attended?"
"What were your favorite courses? Least favorite? Why?"
"Were you promoted while in service? If not, why not?"
"Any particular problems while in the service?"
"What experience did you gain that you feel will be helpful to your future?"

Work experience. Take this one job by job throughout the entire sequence of employment. Here is where you learn whether the applicant is stable or a job hopper. Does the applicant have a history of stability, achievement, ambition, initiative, and cooperativeness? Open up the discussion of each individual job with a broad question: "Tell me about your job with the XYZ Insurance Company." Then probe as deeply as possible with further questions:

"What did you do, specifically?"
"Were you promoted within the company? If not, why not?"
"Tell me about your supervisors."
"Tell me something about the people who worked with you."
"Tell me a little about the company itself."
"Why did you join that particular company?"
"Why did you leave it? (Or why do you want to leave it?)"
"Tell me about the working conditions there."
"If you were managing that company, what would you change?"

Specific interests.

"Why are you applying for work here?"
"What do you know about this company?"
"What specific type of work interests you most?"
"What are your plans for the future?"
"How much do you plan to be earning in five years?"
"Tell me about your hobbies."
"What type of special training do you feel you will need for this job?"
"Describe your plans for career development."
"If you were to change careers, what would you choose? Why?"
"Under what type of working conditions do you work best? Why?"
"Under what type of supervision do you work best? Why?"
"What particular personal characteristics do you have that lend themselves to this job?"
"How will this company benefit from hiring you?"
"What do you expect from this company in return?"

By this time you should have a fairly firm grasp of the applicant's interests, attitudes, capabilities, communicative skills, and social skills. You should be able, at this point, to make a tentative decision on whether you want to hire the applicant, pending results of your follow-up on references, previous employers, educational documentation, and so on.

Be cautious about making a job offer based on interview impressions alone. You don't know yet how much of the information you got is true. If you do make an offer, be certain the applicant understands that it is tentative, pending results of your follow-up for verification.

A word of caution: Be objective. Avoid playing God or psychologist. You are not qualified for either position. You wouldn't believe some of the ridiculous questions managers will ask an applicant, assuming they can derive some deep-seated psychological significance from the replies. One of the best examples I have known was a young manager who insisted on asking an applicant to name his favorite tree. The manager explained, "If the applicant chooses a big sturdy oak, maple, or elm, I know I have an applicant who thinks big. But if he chooses a cherry tree or a flowering mimosa, watch out! That applicant is a weak-minded sissy." Can you imagine anything as asinine as that? Yet perfectly capable people are rejected on such nonsense.

The Application Form

If you don't have a formal employment application form, get one from a local office supply or stationery store. Not only is it good business procedure, it makes good sense. It provides an excellent guide during the interview. Just be certain the application form is legal under present laws relating to hiring.

There are several key things to look for on the application form:

Is it filled out completely, with no blanks?

Is it neat and legible?

Does it present a sequential outline of the applicant's work history, with no unexplained gaps?

Has there been a logical and steady growth in earnings?

Has the applicant stayed with easy jobs or progressed into challenging ones?

Do previous jobs provide related skills that are suitable to your opening?

What about stability? Is the applicant a job hopper?

Why did the applicant leave each job?

Whenever possible, have the application form completed at your location. That is the only way you can be certain the applicant filled it out. Don't laugh! I had a bad experience once. A complete illiterate was hired and that fact wasn't discovered until it was time to fill out the final company insurance application form.

The illiterate employee was promptly terminated. (Fortunately, I wasn't.) The applicant's wife had completed the application form for him at home.

The Reference Check

Here is where you validate the information on the application form and the information you gained during the interview. A personal, face-to-face conversation is the best method of checking references. If not practical, telephone checking is the next best.

Incidentally, personal references are rarely of any value, unless you require no less than ten. If the applicant must list ten references, he may have to dig deeply enough fo find someone who will tell the truth about him. Anyone can list his best friends, neighbors, fraternity brothers, and drinking buddies. And rarely will you get any negative comments from the minister, doctor, or teacher. Why bother going after them?

Your best references are previous employers, especially the applicant's immediate supervisors. They can tell you what you want to know. During your inquiry, include the following questions:

"Specifically, what type of work did he do?"
"How did the applicant get along with his supervisors, peers, and subordinates?"
"What about absenteeism?"
"Did the applicant accept direction well?"
"Why did the applicant leave?"
"If you had an opening and company policy would permit it, would you rehire the applicant? If not, why not?"

Listen to *how* the answers are given. This often conveys a lot of feelings and attitudes.

You will probably have to call the personnel department to verify certain information, and your conversation should go something like this: "This is (your name) with (your company). Mr. Harold Taylor has applied to my company for a position as (the job). Could

I please verify certain information on his application? He said he worked for you from December 1969 until last August. Is that correct? He states that he was earning approximately $450 per week. Is that correct?" (If there is a discrepancy get a full explanation from the applicant.) And his job title was ——? And his reason for leaving? Is there any further information we might find helpful in making our decision?"

Some personnel departments refuse to divulge the information except upon written request. If so, prepare your inquiry on company letterhead stationery and enclose a self-addressed, stamped envelope for the reply.

Never contact a company for which the applicant is still working unless the applicant has given specific permission. To do so would jeopardize the applicant's job and is inexcusable.

Evaluate All the Data

Again, it is important to interview and consider several applicants for each job opening. If you don't, you will find yourself compromising on your selection. Always select the best of several. Review the job specifications and compare them with the applicants' specifications. Pick the candidate who matches best and make the offer. Lay aside all those inaccurate and ridiculous biases such as: "Redheads have a bad temper." "Older people have leveled out and you can't change them." "Younger people are more ambitious and learn faster." "Black people are lazy." "White people expect too much from you." "Women cry when they get angry." "My people won't work well with a woman." These things are sheer nonsense, and could keep you from hiring a potentially productive employee.

Don't let your emotions cloud your better judgment just because a candidate looks good. The question is whether the candidate is qualified, and nothing more. Many poor performers are able to present themselves in a positive way. The very best criterion to follow in employee selection is that if there is any indication of what an employee will do in the future, it is what he has done in the past. Check past performance out religiously. Don't rely solely on appearances. The very qualities that make a good salesman make a good con artist.

Several years ago, an oil company for which I worked was delighted to hire a lubrication engineer who had been working for a major competitor. During the interview, the applicant presented several technical manuals he had written for the competitive company. These added immeasurably to his credentials.

Fortunately, the personnel manager was one who believed in a detailed follow-up on all applicants, regardless of the position in question. It was confirmed that the applicant had worked for the competitive company. However, his period of employment was only two weeks, as a shipping clerk in a warehouse. It was reported that he was terminated for theft. It wasn't until the follow-up that the competitive company was even aware that its technical manuals were missing. The applicant had neither written the manuals nor graduated as an engineer.

A detailed follow-up on all applicants is a must. Undesirable information can be covered up during the interview and omitted from the application form by the applicant. This was well illustrated a few years ago in a company for which I was doing some consulting work. An applicant was being considered for a position in the controller's department. All credentials looked good and there were no significant gaps in his employment record. Upon follow-up, it was learned that his dates of employment with one company did not match the dates on the application form. There was a difference of approximately two years. When he was questioned, the applicant admitted having spent eighteen months in the Missouri State Penitentiary for grand larceny. That's hardly the type of applicant you would consider suitable for a controller's office.

The foregoing cases validate the need for a rigid program of follow-up on *all* applicants. Just remember, on the information you gain from both the application form and the interview—verify,

verify, verify! You're building *your* team and you want a healthy, productive one. Don't rely solely on surface impressions and gut feelings. It isn't worth the gamble.

Evaluation of Supervisory Practices (ESP Rating)

1. Do I plan ahead for hiring needs whenever possible, rather than manage by crisis?
2. Do I have a written job description for each employee in my work group?
3. Do I have a written specification sheet for each job under my supervision?
4. Do I try to avoid using my competitors as a primary source of applicants?
5. Do my employment ads (if used) stand above the roar of others?
6. Am I thoroughly familiar with current laws regarding possible civil rights violations?
7. Do I base my hiring decisions on valid data rather than on gut feelings?
8. Do I listen more than I talk during an interview?
9. Do I follow up with previous employers in all cases in order to validate information?
10. Am I able to lay aside all prejudice and bias when considering an applicant?

3 | Job Descriptions and Performance Standards

Every employee is entitled to know exactly what he is expected to do, how well it is to be done, and how his performance compares against the standards of the job. This statement seems pretty basic and the underlying philosophy will appear several times throughout this book. It is a philosophy with which few managers will argue, yet it is frequently handled in a very cursory manner.

Managers often *assume* that their employees are totally informed about their responsibilities and performance. This is a very dangerous assumption that can be counterproductive within a work group. Time and again I have had managers tell me, "We don't need job descriptions or performance standards. My guys know what they're doing." I have invalidated that statement almost as many times as I have heard it.

I usually find that an employee's perception of the job responsibilities fails to match the manager's perception. I have often interviewed workers in depth to get a detailed outline of their responsibilities as they perceive them. I follow this with an in-depth interview with the manager in order to gain the manager's perception of the workers' responsibilities. Although many similarities surface, there will invariably be significant differences. These differences in perception can have an adverse effect on an employee's performance. Managers who fail to provide detailed job descrip-

50

tions and performance standards are overlooking two important management tools.

Developing the Job Description

Before I get into what a job description is, let me mention what it is not. The job description is not a detailed list of the day-to-day activities of an employee. It is not a description of the tasks he performs on the job. A job description is a list of the things for which the employee is responsible. It is a statement of the responsibilities of the job, not the activities of the job. Even when I find written job descriptions, they are often cluttered with tasks and activities, the things employees *do*.

A few typical responsibilities that might appear in a well-written job description include meeting daily production schedules, operating within a prescribed budget, developing market penetration and coverage, and preparing month-end reports and analyses. These clearly define areas of responsibility, not everyday activities such as typing, answering telephones, driving a truck, checking catalog prices, counting boxes, selling, or filling out forms. These activities are germane to the job, but responsibility is the basis for a job description.

Now that we have separated responsibilities from activities, let's go through a step-by-step procedure for developing a typical job description. You will be able to apply the same principles as you develop descriptions for each job in your group. Just remember to keep the job descriptions simple, clear, and complete. A clear, concise job description is usually no longer than two or three pages, and contains the following key elements: job title, basic job function, relationships, responsibilities, authority, standards of performance, and accountability.

Job title. This is simply the job title as it appears on the organization chart, in personnel records, and in employment advertising—for example, mail-room supervisor, production foreman, accounts payable clerk, territory sales representative, warehouse superintendent, draftsman, or night watchman.

Basic job function. The job function should be stated clearly in one sentence:

Production Foreman. Under the direction of the production manager, the foreman supervises an assigned section of the production department and is responsible for the efficient, safe, and profitable operation of his section.

Materials Manager. The materials manager purchases economically, regulates deliveries of, stores, and distributes all material necessary on the production line.

Territory Sales Representative. The territory sales representative maintains a constantly growing volume, in both coverage and penetration, of profitable sales within his assigned territory.

Mail-Room Supervisor. The mail-room supervisor receives, sorts, and delivers all incoming mail properly, and handles all outgoing mail, including the accurate and timely posting of such mail.

File Clerk. Following established company procedures, the clerk is responsible for the accurate and timely filing of all incoming material, including retrieval of requested files.

Automotive Mechanic. The mechanic is responsible for maintaining proper operation of company vehicles, as assigned by service orders received from the service manager.

Relationships. This statement clearly defines the employee's lines of communications, reporting channels, and expected contacts with others, both inside and outside the organization. It is essentially a written definition of the employee's position within the organization chart, including dotted-line relationships. For example, the relationships of a personnel manager may look something like this:

Reports to: Vice-president of employee relations
Supervises: Personnel clerks, test administrator, personnel file clerk, labor relations director, and one secretary

Works with: All department managers and executive management
Outside the company: Personnel agencies, executive recruiting
   firms, union representatives, state and federal employment
   offices, and various vendors

Responsibilities. Four examples of basic responsibilities were
listed previously. However, this section of the job description
should include *all* the things for which the employee is responsible. Again, list the responsibilities, not the activities through
which the employee meets his responsibilities. The responsibilities are those areas in which the employee's achievements will be
measured.

Typical basic responsibilities for various job assignments include:

Maintaining balanced and controlled inventories
Accurate posting of accounts payable
Maintaining favorable purchase price variances
Repairing production line tools and equipment
Proper and timely delivery of incoming mail
Verifying incoming shipments of materials
Planning, laying out, and regulating flow of work
Selecting, training, and supervising personnel
Maintaining safe operation of all equipment
Maintaining department compliance with standard operating
   procedures (SOP)
Timely reporting of department activities
Determining and correcting errors in accounts receivable invoices
Maintaining timely and smooth flow of both incoming and out-
   going telephone calls
Resolving all customer complaints on a fair and timely basis

An employee engages in many activities in order to meet the
above responsibilities, but those activities should not clutter the
job description.

One item I frequently find that should *never* be included in a
job description is the "cop-out clause"; that is, "other duties, as

assigned." This is no more than a manager's license to misuse his people. It is his way of preventing an employee from saying, "That's not my job." Personally, I feel that any employee should be protected from such misuse. Those of you who were in the army can well remember the cop-out clause in the Articles of War: "conduct unbecoming a soldier." If they couldn't get you on any other article, they could get you on that one. The same is true of "other duties, as assigned." Don't ever let this appear in a job description.

Authority. This section of the job description should define the limits of your delegation to the employee, including his decision-making limitations, budgetary limitations, and direct supervision of other personnel. Typical statements of authority might include:

Approval of purchase requests up to $500

Granting of time off or leaves of absence

Discipline of department personnel, including suspension and termination, within SOP guidelines

Recommendations for salary increases, promotions, and transfers

Interviewing and hiring of new employees, as required within manning tables

Approval of customer service requests up to $100

Approval of customer credit applications

Hiring of temporary help, as required

Removal of unauthorized personnel from the premises

Authority to carry out all activities and to maintain the relationships specified in this job description

Standards of performance. This subject is usually treated as a separate unit but I find it impractical to separate it from the job description. It is a significant part of the job description. Basically, it is a statement of how well the employee is expected to achieve each of the primary responsibilities in the job description. It is the standard against which his performance will be measured. It sets the par for the course so the employee knows at all times how he is progressing toward expectations.

Standards of performance define such things as how well, how often, how soon, how frequently, how accurately, how much, and the allowable margins of error. Standards of performance are similar, and often identical, to goals, as discussed in Chapter 5. Specific goals, however, are usually aimed toward short-term activities on which special emphasis is being placed. Standards of performance are of a more permanent nature in most cases. That is not to say, however, that the standards can't be changed.

A performance standard is a statement of the conditions that will exist when the job has been done to your satisfaction. In other words, it tells the employee what it will look like when it has been done to your satisfaction. Writing standards is not difficult so long as you know what you want or how well you want a job done. And that doesn't mean a nebulous statement like, "Do your best." That says nothing, and establishes absolutely no quality control for the job.

Here is an easy way to go about developing performance standards. Select any one of the responsibilities you included in the employee's job description and complete this sentence regarding that particular responsibility: "I will be completely satisfied with your work when ____." Complete this sentence for each responsibility listed in the job descriptions and you will have a well-defined set of standards.

To get a feel for developing standards, let's take a few of the previously listed responsibilities and set some standards for each of them (not necessarily all-inclusive):

Accurate posting of accounts payable
1. All invoices received are posted within the same working day.
2. All invoices are routed to proper department managers for approval no later than the day following receipt.
3. An average of no more than three posting errors per month occur.
4. Posting ledger is balanced by the end of the third working day of each month.

Meeting daily production schedule
1. Work group produces no less than 426 widgets per working day.
2. No more than an average of 2 percent of widgets is rejected at the next work station.
3. Work is completed with no more than an average of 5 percent overtime per week.

Developing market penetration and coverage
1. Both penetration (market share) and coverage meet or exceed established goals of current market plan.
2. Net increase in new customers is no less than 10 percent per year.
3. Sales volume meets or exceeds goals as established by current market plan.

The standards are not difficult to write if you know how well you want a job done. It's just a matter of defining them for the employee. If you don't know how well you want the job done, you have no right to evaluate the employee's performance. If you don't establish performance standards in writing, you have left the quality control aspect of the job up to the employee. You would have no right to criticize performance.

Please notice what a perfect outline performance standards make for a performance appraisal. The appraisal would only be a matter of going through the standards one by one, and discussing to what degree the standards were met, not met, or exceeded, and why. Standards met become targets for recognition to the employee. Standards missed become targets for improvement, training, or coaching. Well-written performance standards are a little like air conditioning; once you have them you'll never want to be without them. Your employees will feel the same way about them. They will know when they are on target.

From the employee's standpoint much greater interest in the job is generated when good standards are established. The employee knows where he stands at all times. He knows immediately when he is off target. To repeat, every employee is entitled to know exactly what he is expected to do (job description) and how well he is expected to do it (performance standards). When he knows both, your job of managing is much easier, because the employee can manage his own activities better.

Accountability. Although an employee is accountable for every responsibility listed in the job description, this section defines the broad areas of responsibility for which he may be called to task. There will be some obvious overlap, but it serves to highlight those responsibilities considered top priority in management's eyes. For example, a production foreman might be accountable to the production manager for the production schedule, quality standards, absenteeism and tardiness, employee turnover, cost controls, and safety and loss-time accidents within the group. The accountability for a retail sales clerk might include accuracy of sales transactions, safeguarding of company funds, equipment, and inventory, maintenance of favorable customer relations, control of absenteeism, and maintenance of adequate shelf inventories.

In summary, job descriptions are not difficult to write if you know what you want done and how well you want it done. Get your employees involved in developing their own job descriptions. They know their jobs well. There is nothing wrong in getting the input of an employee in setting performance standards either. Ask the employee to write the standards he feels would be realistic, the standards against which he feels he should be measured. An employee who has held a specific job for any reasonable period of time is usually able to develop a fine job description if given the guidelines of this chapter.

Job descriptions are not static. Jobs change, so job descriptions must change. They should be reviewed every year or two and re-written if necessary. The performance standards might have to be raised or lowered. Authority and accountability may need to be updated. If job descriptions are current, employee output is likely to meet current expectations.

Evaluation Of Supervisory Practices (ESP Rating)

1. Have I discussed job responsibilities with each of my employees to be certain their perception of the job matches mine?
2. Are the job descriptions of my people broken down into key areas of responsibility, rather than tasks or activities?
3. Have I avoided the "cop-out clause" in all job descriptions?
4. Have I defined each employee's limits of authority clearly?
5. Do I have clear-cut standards of performance developed for each key responsibility?
6. Does each of my employees understand thoroughly what I consider satisfactory performance?
7. Do I use performance standards as a guide during performance appraisals?
8. Do I have each employee help me develop his own job description and performance standards?
9. Do I keep all job descriptions and performance standards current?
10. Does each employee have (or have available at all times) a copy of his job description?

4 | New Employee Orientation

Employee orientation actually begins the minute an applicant walks in the front door of your company facility, be it an office, a warehouse, a production plant, or any other work location. It is essential that the applicant gain a favorable impression of your company at the outset. The impression he gets will determine the applicant's initial feeling toward your company. He should have a positive attitude toward the possibility of working with your organization. The first contact is very important, and usually begins with the receptionist. It sets the stage for everything to come.

Just a few months ago, I witnessed perhaps the most flagrant violation of initial orientation I have ever seen. I was sitting in the reception lobby of a manufacturing plant, waiting to keep an appointment with the general manager. As I sat there thumbing through a trade magazine, a young man walked up to the receptionist and inquired about any possible job openings. The sequence of events violated every rule in the book regarding the handling of applicants.

The receptionist, typically, was handling the switchboard, stuffing envelopes, making appointments, drinking coffee, and making a vain attempt at polishing her nails. When the applicant inquired about job openings, she didn't even look up or offer any kind of greeting. Through a well-learned pattern of conditioned reflexes, she handed him an application form and told him to sit down in the lobby and fill it out. No pencil or pen was offered. Fortunately, the poor guy had a stubby pencil, but it had no eraser.

A couple of chairs were vacant but the only writing surface was an eighteen-inch-high coffee table, covered with trade magazines and completely filled ashtrays. The young man pushed enough magazines aside to gain some table space and began to fill out the application form. His posture at that point would have been suitable for tying his shoelaces.

At one point, I noticed he paused quite a while and looked around the lobby several times. As he did, I glanced down at his half-completed application. He was listing all his previous places of employment, but could remember neither the complete addresses nor the telephone numbers. You guessed it! There was no telephone directory in the room to help him. I watched as he turned the incomplete application in to the receptionist. Without looking up, she laid the form in a file basket and replied with a mechanical "We'll give you a call if anything comes up." Whereupon the young man left.

What kind of impression would this man have of a company that treated him in such an indifferent and cold manner? Why would he want to work for such a company? Although this situation is unusual, it happens.

First impressions are extremely important and are usually lasting, so be certain they are positive. You may have to provide some special training for your receptionist. If so, do it. Otherwise your receptionist may cost you some potentially productive employees. Every applicant is entitled to be treated with honesty, courtesy, and dignity. If handled properly, a new employee will have a positive attitude toward you and your company as well as toward the work situation.

Once the employee has been hired, the final employment papers have been completed, and the company benefit programs have been explained, it is time to orient the employee to the job. At this point, it is extremely important to recognize the employee's state of mind. In this totally new situation, the employee feels out of place, socially unaccepted, confused, and worried as to whether he will perform well. He is also wondering how the work group will accept him. Even a newly hired corporate vice-president feels this way at first. It is essential that an employee orientation procedure be followed that will ease the new employee's anxiety and give him the feeling that the company and the other employees are genuinely concerned about him. The new staff member must be made to feel welcome.

The first step is to introduce the employee to his work group. Take, don't send, the employee to the group and introduce him to everyone there, especially the group leader or supervisor. Tell the group something about the employee's background and why he was selected for the job. Explain fully to the employee the job functions and safety regulations, to whom he will report, and where necessary tools and materials are obtained. Answer any questions he may have. Try to see that he gets a favorable impression of the job, the group, and the company. The employee should also be introduced to other key personnel, especially to those with whom he will need to come in contact. You may wish to introduce him to key personnel before taking him to the specific work group.

The buddy system can be very effective in making employee orientation more effective. Appoint another member of the work group as the new employee's buddy, someone who will periodically ask him how things are going or whether there is anything he can help him with or questions he can answer. Frequent follow-up on your part will be very important at first. It lets the employee know you are interested in him. The "buddy" can be helpful in getting him adjusted socially by accompanying him to lunch the first few days and arranging for some contact with other employees. The assigned buddy can also advise you of any special problems, problems the new man may be reluctant to bring to you personally.

The employee should be given a copy of his written job description, including a thorough discussion of everything in it. Let him know you don't expect perfection at first and that everyone will do everything possible to help him learn the job. Go over the performance standards of the job, with a full explanation of what is expected. It is important that the employee understand fully the standards by which he will be measured.

Go over in detail the training he will get to help him learn the job and the future training he can expect to promote career development. Furnish the employee any pertinent references, books, or manuals that must be studied.

First impressions are important impressions. Be certain the new staff member is favorably impressed. He comes to the job with some very important things on his mind:

> "I want to feel like an important part of this organization, not just another cog in the wheel."
>
> "I want to know exactly what I am expected to do, and how well I am expected to do it."
>
> "I want to know what help I will get in learning to do my job well."
>
> "I want to know to whom I should turn for help, answers, and encouragement."
>
> "I want to know the rules, regulations, and policies I am expected to know."
>
> "I want to contribute something important."
>
> "I want to be accepted by all."

It is your responsibility, as manager, to see that all of these employee's "wants" are satisfied. That is the reason for the new employee orientation. You may find it helpful to develop and use a new employee orientation checklist like the one shown as Figure 3, to be certain all bases are covered during the orientation. This checklist, of course, must be customized to the job.

Evaluation of Supervisory Practices (ESP Rating)

1. Has my secretary or receptionist been thoroughly instructed on how to meet and treat all applicants and visitors?

NEW EMPLOYEE ORIENTATION

☐ Employment papers completed

☐ Company benefit booklets presented and explained

☐ Discuss job description and performance standards

☐ Discuss safe working procedures

☐ Discuss company regulations and policies

☐ Explain complaint and/or grievance procedures

☐ Discuss days and hours of work and/or training

☐ Discuss complete training program and procedure

☐ Discuss lines of communications/authority

☐ Present and discuss appropriate references, manuals, books, etc.

☐ Introduce to key company personnel

☐ Introduce to specific work group

☐ Question and answer period for employee

Figure 3. New employee orientation checklist.

2. Would a walk-in applicant gain a favorable first impression of my company?
3. Do I have a thorough, step-by-step procedure for conducting a new employee orientation?
4. Do I personally introduce each new employee to the people with whom he will be working?
5. Do I use a "buddy system" as part of my employee orientation program?

5 | Responsibility, Authority, and Accountability

Under the contractual arrangement presented in Chapter 1, your objective is to gain employee commitment to goals and objectives. If the employee is to develop a sense of ownership in the objectives of your work group, you are going to have to meet your obligations under the contract; that is, delegate certain elements of the job. If you were able to do the entire job of the work group, you wouldn't have employees. Each is expected to assume certain job functions and bring them to completion.

But delegation doesn't mean passing along only the distasteful jobs, the menial tasks, the hard labor, and the unenjoyable slices of activity. It doesn't mean the manager keeps all the "fun" tasks and deals the others out among the employees.

Delegation is the logical, objective, and rational division of a total workload into manageable and challenging units. Those units are then put into the hands of employees in their entirety, with all the tools necessary to get the job done. Unless an entire unit is delegated, the employee will feel he has only a part of a job, and will not feel very committed. I am not implying that full delegation is possible with a new employee. Naturally, competence must be present.

The human animal is an achieving beast. Every last one of us senses a great satisfaction in achieving, in accomplishing something worthwhile, in bringing a project to a successful completion, no matter how simple or complex the project might be. A job well done gives a great sense of accomplishment. How can an employee develop such a sense from completing part of a job?

Yet I have seen managers delegate parts of jobs and expect great motivational returns, high levels of achievement, and quality output. These managers probably wonder why their employees aren't growing in their jobs and developing the capacity for assuming even more responsibility. One cannot grow until one is given the opportunity to stretch.

A typical analogy has developed in many households. How often has a child begged for a puppy as a pet, and promised to care for it, feed it, train it, housebreak it, clean up the messes, and even pay for the dog food. The majority of these children soon learned that if they neglected the distasteful or time-consuming aspects of pet care, good old mom and dad would take over for them. Frankly, the children did a better job of delegating than the parents. The jobs were delegated "up."

What kind of responsibility did these children learn? What sense of achievement did they have? Much more would have been gained, from a growth standpoint, if the entire responsibility had been delegated—and managed. The only problem was, the children were typical managers. They kept the "fun" parts and delegated the hard labor. But will they grow into responsible adults as a result of this type of learning experience? Not if this educational pattern continues.

On the job it is essential that you delegate a job in its entirety, including full responsibility for completion. When you do, it gives the employee a better perspective. The job becomes his project, his activity. The employee will be able to say, "I did it!" This alone becomes his motivation to achieve even more. There was a commitment to a project that belonged to the employee.

An old story well illustrates the different perspectives employees have of their jobs. A man was walking down the sidewalk when he came upon a group of construction workers on a project. He asked three men what they were doing. One said, "I'm laying bricks." Another said, "I'm building a wall." The third worker laid down his trowel, stepped back, looked up at the project, and said, "Sir, I'm building a cathedral!" It was obvious which worker felt a sense of ownership in the project. It's also obvious who will have the greatest pride in seeing the cathedral completed. This sense of ownership is what you, the manager, must develop in each of your people.

To quote a young lady in a television commercial a few years ago, "Mother, please, I'd rather do it myself!" We *want* challenging experiences. We want to get things done. We want to feel a sense of ownership in our work. We want to enjoy the sense of achievement, of accomplishment.

Think of the confidence you would be showing in one of your employees if you said, "Phil, here's a project we want to see completed by the end of the month. I'm sure you can handle it, so I'm putting it entirely in your hands. It's your baby and I'm going to let you handle the entire responsibility. Just let me know if there is any help you need. And when you finish it, I would like for you to present it to management."

That puts the ball squarely in Phil's court. It's all his, and he knows it. Not only will he experience the satisfaction of completing the project, he knows he will get the credit for achievement. Motivation? You bet! Give him a sweet taste of responsibility and he'll come back for more. This is how employees grow and develop.

Responsibility means decision making, too, even at the cost of mistakes. Naturally, there are limitations on what decisions can be delegated, but probably more of it could be delegated than managers are willing to admit. Some managers underrate the intelligence of their employees. Other managers can't resist the parental urge to make everyone's decisions for them. They feel more secure when employees have to come running to them for decisions. They feel it is the only way to retain control. But employees who are never given opportunities to make decisions will never develop the needed skills. Failure to delegate in the full sense of the word leaves a terrible void in any program of employee growth and development.

By no means does delegation connote abdication of your management responsibility. Obviously you can't turn everything over to employees. Different employees have different levels of skills and knowledge. Some have more experience. Some willingly accept more responsibility than others. They have different workloads. But if the project is within the scope of the employee's ability, delegate it—all of it.

Setting Goals

One of the most effective ways of gaining employee commitment is to let the employee have a voice in setting his work objectives. This is another of the key reasons management by objectives, or participative management, has been so successful. The employees have a voice in determining the objectives they are expected to achieve. When a manager works with each of his employees in establishing work goals, it strengthens the supervisor/subordinate relationship, gains employee commitment, and usually produces better results than dictated objectives will produce.

Goal setting is one of the responsibilities your employees will welcome. They want to have a voice in it. It shows faith in their intelligence. It's a source of recognition to have their opinions respected, and it gives them a feeling of importance. It enhances their self-image. They want this responsibility. Let's face it, the employees are closer to the job and understand its potential far better than someone farther up the corporate ladder. You and your employees should know more about the potential productivity of your individual work group than anyone else in your company.

As a manager yourself, responsible to those above you in the organization, you are well aware of the motivational effect of being involved in establishing your objectives. You like to be involved. You want your input respected. You want a part of the action, and when you get it you feel a deeper sense of commitment to company objectives. Your people feel the same way. Let them be a part of your planning.

There are two primary reasons why more participative management isn't seen. First is the old "erroneous concept of others" suffered by so many managers. They underestimate the intelligence of their employees, feel they aren't capable of thinking or planning, and feel no particular need to gain their input. The second is laziness. It takes time and work to have employees participate in establishing work goals. It is so much easier and faster simply to assign or dictate objectives to employees. Sure, it's easier, but it fails to gain employee commitment toward attainment. There is no sense of ownership in the goals. Employees have been denied a much needed sense of responsibility in what is to be achieved.

Participation in goal setting can be a reality in virtually every level of an organization, from the top of the chart to the bottom. The lower you go on the organization chart the greater the participation because more people and more organizational units are involved. Conversely, the higher up you go, the less the participation.

Objectives established at top corporate levels are vague and general by design. They are overall targets that must be achieved to sustain corporate growth and earnings. Typical targets are production output, cost reductions, research projects, sales volume, and profit contributions. Corporate management well knows what it must have in order to sustain company growth and earnings. These overall goals must be established and announced.

All other objectives established throughout the organization must make specific contributions toward the achievement of the corporate objectives. The farther down the organization we go, the more detailed and specific the objectives become. Every work group and individual in the company must establish personal objectives that contribute to the overall corporate objectives. The sum of the individual objectives must equal or exceed the corporate objectives.

Every subdivision of the corporation is responsible for its contribution to the overall goals, whether they be increases, such as sales, earnings, volume, output, or projects, or decreases, such as scrap, costs, materials, injuries, theft, absenteeism, or employee turnover. But no one is more capable of determining what a work group can accomplish than the people who make up that work group, including their manager. Remember the old adage, "None of us is as smart as all of us."

Sit down with each of your employees and discuss his job. Ask for his suggestions in establishing objectives. A word of caution, however: Employees tend to set higher objectives for themselves than management would have set. It may require some tactful discussion to bring the objectives to a realistic level.

Your employees are eager to make a good impression on you; they may tend to let their enthusiasm overload their objectives. Achievement-oriented people, in particular, tend to overestimate what they can accomplish. As their manager, it will be up to you to determine whether their objectives are realistic and attainable. If not, they must be reduced to realistic levels.

In discussing objectives with an employee or work group, there are two key questions to pose: "What do you feel you can achieve?" "How do you plan to do it?" Many other questions must be asked, of course, but you want the employee to think, analyze, and plan how and what he is capable of achieving during the ensuing month, quarter, or year. Both long-term and short-term objectives must be considered. The employee must know where he can be one year hence (objective), and plan a course of action to get there.

Every objective must be reviewed periodically, by both the manager and the employee, to see whether conditions dictate adjustment. Market conditions, raw materials supply, or workloads can change, and labor disputes or employee turnover can disrupt operations. A host of things can happen that require adjustment in both individual and group objectives.

Let's take a look at the criteria of a well-stated objective. It should contain five essential elements:

1. *Realistic and attainable.* An objective that is obviously so high it cannot be reached becomes a demoralizing and demotivating factor, and the employee will not reach for it. This often causes productivity to drop rather than increase. The employee quickly develops a "why try?" attitude and productivity suffers. On the other hand, if objectives are unrealistically low, they promote laziness and indifference, and the employee may turn idle time toward noncompany activities.

2. *Provides stretch.* The objective must cause the employee to work a little harder, longer, or smarter to reach it than he would to achieve a goal requiring "average" efforts. This is the only way the employee can grow and provide the increased output necessary for corporate growth.

3. *Clearly and unambiguously stated.* Clear and unambiguously stated goals are necessary in order to avoid any misunderstanding on the part of either the manager or the employee concerning exactly what is to be achieved. They make the objective clear for everyone, an important factor in avoiding future arguments about what was to be achieved.

4. *Measurable.* The objective must be measurable in terms of numbers, dollars, units, time factor, outputs, reductions, increases, or other factors. Unless it is measurable, you will never know whether it was achieved. If the objective cannot be measured (other than by opinion), you may be faced with the responsibility of proving that you are accomplishing anything at all.

5. *Written down.* Recording the objective in writing will eliminate any future misunderstanding as to what was to be achieved. It further gains the personal commitments of the employee and his manager.

Unfortunately, a manager's first efforts at participative objective setting often prove disappointing. If this happens, don't give up and start dictating objectives. Teach your employees how to set objectives properly. It is a skill that can and should be acquired.

An employee's personal objective often turns out to be no more than a nice, laudable statement of good intentions: "During the coming year I will exercise greater diligence in the performance of my duties, and will expend greater effort in increasing my corporate contribution." That's a wonderful thought, but it is certainly no well-stated personal objective.

Every objective should meet the five criteria stated earlier. Consider the following:

"By June 1 I will have increased my production of widgets to an average of 200 per hour, with no more than 1 percent rejections at the next work station."

"By year-end my total sales volume will have increased no less than 6 percent over the previous year, and I will have added at least seven new customers to my sales territory."

"By December 31 the annual operating costs of my department will not have exceeded $52,000, and employee turnover will not be greater than 4 percent."

"By the end of this fiscal year, we will have reduced industrial accidents in this department by no less than 20 percent compared with the previous year."

These objectives are clearly stated, specific, and absolutely measurable. We would have to assume they are realistic and would provide "stretch" for the people concerned.

Each objective carries an element of risk—the risk that it may not be attained. Any specifically stated objective should include this risk. It develops a deeper commitment to achievement. An employee understands that his performance will be measured in terms of achievement. He further understands that his achievement will have a direct bearing on promotions, salary increases, opportunities, and special privileges. Conversely, failure to achieve or failure to meet objectives will have a negative effect on his progress. This he also understands.

Once an employee has committed himself to an objective, with its element of risk, he will work harder to achieve it in order to avoid the negative consequences of failure. But don't allow employees to include a "weasel factor" in their objectives. They will invariably try to build in escape clauses to protect themselves if the objective is not met. Consider the following:

> During the next six months I will increase my territorial sales by no less than 8 percent *if* we have good weather, *if* the advertising department comes through, and *if* no product shortages develop.

If the sales representative doesn't meet the objective, he can weasel out of the responsibility by blaming someone else. Don't let it happen. Keep the weasel factor out of stated objectives. If the escape clause is included, it diminishes the employee's sense of responsibility. Conveying this sense of responsibility is one of *your* objectives.

Sit down with the employee, go over the job description, and pick out the key responsibilities of the job. Work with the employee in setting objectives in each key responsibility. Be certain each objective meets the five criteria stated earlier, with no weasel factors included.

Both you and the employee must be able to justify objectives you feel are realistic and attainable. It will usually be necessary for you to reconcile your differences of opinion before objectives are mutually agreed on. However, in the final analysis you, the manager, must make the decision when disagreement develops. Just be fair and realistic. It will pay big rewards for the employee, for you, and for your company. The important thing is, it gives the employee a piece of the action, a sense of ownership, a feeling of responsibility, and a personal commitment.

In a sense, well-stated objectives are performance standards. They not only state what will be achieved, but also describe how soon, how completely, and how much. When such objectives are clearly established at the beginning of the month, quarter, or year, the employee knows exactly the standards against which his performance will be measured. The employee will be able to plot progress against those standards and will know without any doubt whether his progress is following a successful pattern.

Authority

Here's another place where you will have to "cut the cord" to some extent. If an employee is to be held responsible for meeting objectives, he must be given the tools necessary to get the job done. That includes the authority to make some decisions. The employee's sense of ownership is diminished greatly if he must come to you for all decisions affecting the outcome of his delegated activities.

Avoid the parental instinct to think for your people. Delegate certain decision making, even at the risk of a few cases of misjudgment. If you, for example, have the authority to give final approval for requisitions up to $500, why not allow subordinates to make their own decisions up to, perhaps, $50 or $100? This is only an example, but it serves to illustrate the delegation of authority. Don't worry, things won't go into a state of chaos. Your people won't sell you out. They won't give away the store when they are given some authority in decision making. They develop a sense of responsibility for the outcome. That's what you want. It also gives you more time to make bigger decisions and to perform other management tasks.

For your particular work group, you can find many areas in which decision making can be delegated. As you are working with an employee to establish objectives, ask the employee what authority he really needs to get the job done. Go over the employee's job description, searching for areas in which decision-making authority might help. You will probably find several. Here are some examples that may spark your thinking:

Interviewing and hiring employees
Terminating employees when necessary
Handling grievances
Handling disciplinary procedures
Granting time off
Approving requisitions
Approving service or parts requests

Purchasing materials and equipment
Contracting for services
Entertaining customers
Granting overtime
Handling direct contact with other departments
Reorganizing work area, office, or warehouse

Another way of determining what authority to delegate is to analyze questions brought to you by your employees. Are they coming to you for decisions they should be making? Could you allow
some latitude in these decisions? Such questions may be consuming more of your time than you thought. They are also taking up
the employees' time, as they trot back and forth to get decisions
they could make themselves. Think about it.

I once worked with a sales manager who had asked for some
help in time management and work organization. He said he simply didn't have enough time to get all his work done and was fall-
ing behind. As a result, part of his work was poorly done and part
was never done. His manager had pointed this out to him rather
sternly. That's when the sales manager asked for help.

I spent two days with him, silently sitting in his office, observing and taking notes on his activities. There were several obvious
areas needing improvement, but I found the one factor that was
consuming most of his day.

He had four in-house salesmen working for him who constantly
came to him for decisions and the answers to a multitude of questions. I began to jot down each question they posed. By the end
of two days I had written more than forty questions.

As I went over the questions with him, I asked two questions:
"How many of these questions could the salesmen have answered
themselves if you weren't here and they felt they could make a
decision in your absence?" and "What authorities could you delegate to these salesmen that would eliminate their need to come to
you so often?" With careful analysis, he found that three-fourths of
the questions could have been avoided if the salesmen had been
given minimum latitude in making decisions. The salesmen and

the sales manager were all wasting valuable time in unnecessary conversation, time that could have been used more productively.

The manager broke the job down into logical increments and delegated several specific authorities to the salesmen. They were delighted, and the manager gained some very valuable time he could use for management functions that had been neglected.

Managers who fail to delegate properly tend to become activity fanatics. That is, they tend to concentrate on managing their employees' activities and often lose sight of the objectives those activities were designed to produce. This type of management is terribly time-consuming and dilutes the manager's effectiveness. The manager seems to spend the majority of his time putting out fires, and rarely realizes that he is the one with the match. Proper delegation to capable employees with all the necessary responsibility and authority that go with it actually reduces the manager's workload. It also produces greater results.

Accountability

Accountability for results is an important aspect of any job. Earlier we discussed the element of risk when objectives are not met, and this element of risk can certainly provide the challenge for attainment. Challenge makes any job more interesting and it should be an inherent part of any assignment.

If an employee feels a sense of ownership in, or commitment to, an objective, that employee will also feel a responsibility for reaching it, including an acceptance of the element of risk. Without accountability, the pride of achievement is diminished. If an employee knows he will get the credit for results achieved, that employee readily accepts the risk of discredit for failure and will work harder to avoid failure when both elements—credit and discredit— are present. If an employee is responsible for producing a result, he must be accountable for that result. This should be firmly established in no uncertain terms at the moment of delegation.

Does all this mean an employee is to be fired if the objective isn't reached? Of course not, but it plants another entry of "nonperformance" in the employee's record, to be considered along with other factors in determining salary increases, promotions, transfers, and so on. Both performance and nonperformance factors should be included in any employee's records. This should be firmly understood by the employee. The performance and nonperformance factors accumulated in an employee's file provide important ammunition for his next performance appraisal. They are a written record of what was or was not achieved.

As a manager, you are accountable for the achievement of certain corporate objectives. You will be called to task if they are not achieved. This accountability is no more than the sum of accountabilities of your employees. Let each shoulder his share of the accountability. But don't expect accountability unless you have also delegated clear-cut authority for achievement. Don't expect an employee to build you a cathedral with half a set of tools. It's all one package, and that package includes all the help you can give to your employees in helping them meet their objectives.

When responsibility, authority, and accountability are placed squarely in the lap of an employee, the odds for achievement are substantially improved. The employee has the gut feeling, "It's mine. I'm responsible for it. I'll do it." This sense of ownership is the personal commitment you want felt by all employees toward all objectives. When you have it, you have a productive team.

It goes without saying that the employee must have the skills and knowledge to do the job, or delegation will be no less than disastrous. Failure to delegate, however, is seldom based on the employee's inability to do the job. It is usually based on the manager's erroneous concept of the employee's judgment or the manager's parental tendency to keep control. If you are not delegating properly and thoroughly, just be certain your rationale is objective and justified, and not selfish in nature.

Accountability is established through performance standards and clearly stated objectives, as discussed earlier in this chapter. Accountability for specific or special assignments is clearly established at the time of assignment. An employee must understand in no uncertain terms exactly what is to be accomplished, how well it is to be done, how soon, how completely, and the standard by which achievement is to be evaluated. This information, coupled with the necessary responsibility and authority to get the job done and a manager's honest faith in the employee, will produce results beyond most managers' expectations.

Evaluation of Supervisory Practices (ESP Rating)

1. Do I make it a point to delegate some of the parts of the job that are really *my* favorites?
2. Do I delegate complete, manageable, and challenging units of the workload, rather than bits and pieces?
3. Do I establish full accountability for accomplishment at the time of delegation?
4. Do I delegate as much decision making as I should?
5. Do my employees work with me in establishing individual and group objectives or goals?
6. Regarding delegation, do I trust my employees to the extent to which I want my supervisor to trust me?
7. Do I avoid dictating objectives just to save time?
8. Do I adjust objectives periodically as conditions dictate?
9. Are all employees' objectives realistic and attainable?
10. Do all objectives provide "stretch" for my employees?
11. Does each employee's understanding of what is to be accomplished match mine?
12. Have I removed all "weasel factors" from the objectives?
13. Do I delegate as much authority as my employees need in order to achieve their objectives?
14. Do I give full credit for objectives met?

6 | Training Employees

Nowhere among your managerial responsibilities will you find one of greater impact than that of training and developing your employees. Only through them are you able to multiply your efforts toward achieving corporate objectives. Yet this is one area of management in which we see the weakest efforts being applied, when applied at all.

It is too easy for managers to fall into the "experience trap"; that is, to hire people with experience and not train them. That is no less than blindness and sheer abdication of responsibility. Whether an employee has one year or twenty years of experience, that employee will always need training and development. Markets change, people change, conditions change, processes change, materials change, procedures change. So people must constantly change.

When you hire an employee with twenty years of experience, you really aren't sure whether that person has twenty years' of experience, or one year's experience twenty times. Sure, you want to hire people with as many of the required job skills as possible, but there will always be further training or retraining required.

If you are fortunate enough to have a professional corporate trainer to help you do the job, so much the better. Few managers are so fortunate. But even if you do have access to such a person, in no way does this relieve you of the direct responsibility for training your people. It will always be 100 percent your responsibility. The professional trainer is there to help you do the job better, not to do it for you.

Let's set our thinking straight before we go any farther. Some people cringe at the word "training" in the context in which it is being used here. These people are somewhat sophisticated in their thinking, perhaps rightly so, when they say, "Training is what you do to monkeys; development is what you do to people." The point won't be argued here. There is no purpose served by getting into a semantic argument over the difference. I certainly recognize that a difference exists between the two, but it has nothing to do with monkeys.

Training is a very specialized and practical form of education. Basically, training prepares employees to do their jobs well in the following ways: (1) by teaching the skills necessary for efficient work habits and a high degree of craftsmanship; (2) by building knowledge that makes for logical, intelligent action and decisions; and (3) by forming attitudes that promote cooperation and coordination with other employees and with management. Training is aimed at specific job-related skills and techniques that can be learned in a measurable manner and used on the job. These skills may be better described as observable skills.

Development usually relates to the long-term growth and preparation of the employee for managerial and executive levels of the organization, or perhaps to development of the total organization. The important difference is that development is a broadening experience for the individual and it is designed to increase the person's strengths, such as mental awareness, decision-making and planning capabilities, and the ability to combine experiences and responsibilities into a meaningful relationship.

Training traditionally faces a problem. Management is frequently forced to plunge employees directly into the work, permitting them to make errors, learn by mistakes, and absorb what they can during the process. They learn mostly by osmosis and observation. This unfortunate situation usually means management has failed to plan ahead regarding personnel requirements. When it is managing by crisis, time pressures override the need for training and the employee is plunged into the job. This happens more frequently in companies that do not have a professional or ongoing training program.

Another typical case is the employee who is promoted into a supervisory or management position without having been trained prior to the assignment. He is expected to learn as he goes, or his manager may intend to train the new supervisor as soon as he can get around to it. On-the-job training is excellent, but not unless it is supplemented with some personal effort on the part of the manager. On-the-job training must have very close supervision.

Training is not something that should be done only once in a while as particular problems develop. It should not be done only for new employees, as in orientation training. Most companies depend heavily on on-the-job training, but an ongoing, planned system is more effective. The total effort should ensure that all employees learn those skills, abilities, and attitudes that will contribute to their welfare and to the welfare of the company.

Thus, emphasis should be placed on all aspects of training. Learning is an ongoing process throughout the life of each person. Therefore, training or the direction of this learning process must also be ongoing. To be effective and to accomplish the desired results, training must be planned just like a production schedule. Effective training is vital to all types and levels of employees in every business situation, because of the need to form coordinated and controlled work groups. Training can help you develop work groups that are united in working toward the common goals of your organization or of the work group itself.

Each work group within your company requires different skills and knowledge. The sales manager must teach such skills as communication, selling, work organization, time management, market research, gaining market coverage and penetration, and handling of customer complaints. There is also a host of knowledge that must be acquired by the sales personnel.

A mass of knowledge and skills must also be taught by materials managers, office managers, production managers, and other supervisors. Each is responsible for the development and training of those employees reporting directly to him. Training is needed in *every* work group, regardless of size.

All too often training gets no more than lip service and falls victim to many pitfalls. We accept the logical and moral aspect of training, and few of us argue against training in the industrial or business environment. Training is as American as apple pie; yet, because of its widespread acceptance, it is one of the most misunderstood and possibly misused of the managerial techniques for increasing efficiency.

If is often hard to find a handle on the need for training. In many instances business efforts are hard to measure, and training seems difficult to evaluate and justify on the budget sheet. Consequently many managers say training is important but fail to do anything about it. The pattern is all too common. A supervisor emphasizes training during the orientation discussions with a new employee, encourages the employee to apply himself with vigor, and indicates that those who learn quickly and produce will surely get ahead. Then the supervisor takes the new employee to some other employee, with an introduction something like, "Harold, this is Jim. Show him the ropes. Let me know if you have any problem today, Harold; we've got to keep things moving!" In effect this supervisor is washing his hands of the training responsibilities for the new employee.

Another problem of the lip service to training is that although training is the best and most logical approach to solving problems related to the lack of skill, knowledge, and morale by workers, it is not a cure-all for all problems and ills. In our sincere effort to get on the industrial training bandwagon, we must not overreact and direct training efforts where they might not even be needed.

Throughout this chapter we will emphasize the careful planning needed for your training activities. Your job is to assure yourself that employees have the knowledge, skills, and attributes to perform their jobs at least in a satisfactory manner and to strive for greater productivity. Keep your training effort simple and related directly to your department's responsibilities and job tasks.

Some Do's and Don'ts of Training

Don't:

Don't assume that all people learn at the same pace. Be patient! You may have to demonstrate a skill several times before it is learned.

Don't feel that a task is easy to learn just because you found it easy. We all find certain skills difficult to learn. Be patient with a new learner.

Don't assume an employee will continue to do something the way you demonstrated it. Skills slip, and you will have to retrain some people.

Don't assume the employee knows how to do something well just because he has had experience. It could be experience in doing it incorrectly.

Don't demand perfection too soon. It takes time for a good habit to develop. Be patient—and encouraging.

Don't *act* interested in your subordinate's learning; *be* interested. A supervisor can look only as good as the employees make him look. They are a reflection of his competence.

Don't ridicule an employee for making a mistake. Let his mistakes become learning experiences. You learned from mistakes, too.

Do:

Do let employees know you expect them to continue doing things correctly.

Do let them know you are always willing to help them learn.

Do follow the five-step method of teaching, as presented in this chapter.

Do give positive recognition for skills learned.

Do keep employees informed, constantly and regularly, on how well they are doing and where they need to improve.

Do ask employees, often, what you can do to help them do a better job.

The Performance Gap

Many experienced employees perform with a high degree of skills and knowledge, especially those who are achievement oriented. But newly hired employees rarely have the required skills to achieve full mastery of the job. There will be a difference between the employee's performance and expected performance, due to his lack of skills and knowledge. The difference between the level of skills and knowledge the employee can demonstrate and the level that would be considered satisfactory (or full mastery of the job) is the employee's performance gap (see Figure 4).

As a manager or supervisor, you are completely responsible for closing the performance gap and bringing the employee's performance up to standard or satisfactory performance. Obviously two things are required.

1. Determining, through demonstration or testing, that the employee does know how to perform certain tasks properly (identifying the performance gap).

2. Thoroughly teaching the skills or knowledge the employee does not have, until he can close the performance gap satisfactorily.

As the employee's manager, you well know the various skills required to do the complete job satisfactorily. *Test* every last one of them. Otherwise you could either waste a lot of time teaching the employee something he already knows or allow the employee to continue on the job in an unsatisfactory manner.

Active Versus Passive Learning

You are working with adult employees. Therefore, before planning any training it is important that you understand a little about the adult learning process. Adults do not learn the same way children do, yet we often see managers attempting to educate their employees the way they would third graders.

PERFORMANCE
CONSIDERED
SATISFACTORY

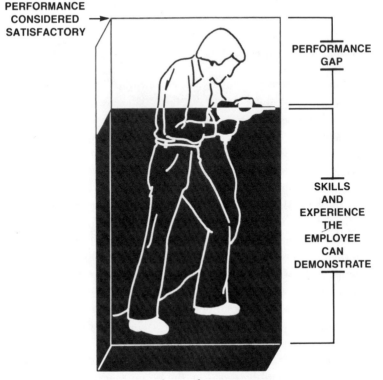

PERFORMANCE
GAP

SKILLS
AND
EXPERIENCE
THE
EMPLOYEE
CAN
DEMONSTRATE

Figure 4. The performance gap.

Children are *passive* learners. They are taught to sit quietly, absorb the information, and regurgitate it upon command. The child often sees no relevance whatsoever to what he is required to endure. His only justification is, "You'll need this later in life." Fortunately, the poor kid accepts this rationale—sits, absorbs and regurgitates on command. He really doesn't know any better.

The child's every movement is planned to be executed on a schedule of commands. He accepts it simply because it's done that way. He isn't old enough to challenge the system. He's told when to get up, when to catch the bus, when to sit down, when to listen, when to write, when to read, and when to speak. Furthermore, his bladder activity is programmed to function at the ring of a recess bell. It's a robot system he accepts because he thinks the world functions that way. He is an excellent example of Pavlov's conditioned reflex.

Adult learning is another story. Rather than submitting to the passive learning process of a child, the adult demands *active* learning that is relevant, busy, and participative.

Unless the adult sees the training as relevant to him, your teaching efforts will not accomplish much. There must be a perceivable payback to the employee. The employee faces the training with one big question in mind: "What's in it for me?" He must see a direct and personal benefit from the training or he will have no reason or inclination to absorb it.

Relevancy must be established by explaining thoroughly why the training is being given, how it will benefit the employee, and why it is important to the work group's productivity. Don't assume relevancy; establish it firmly through a discussion with the employee. Managers often brush over this important phase with some nebulous statement like, "This will be important to your future with the company." That's like telling a child to eat his spinach because it's good for him. The child is disciplined to accept that kind of rationale. An adult will readily reject it, and the training may be largely ignored.

Adults learn by doing. There should be as much activity as possible throughout the learning process. Adults detest lectures, especially those delivered by corporate executives who think they are imparting information. There is a great difference between teaching and telling.

Adults want to be involved in the learning process: doing, practicing, manipulating, experimenting, and moving around. They find it both challenging and stimulating. Involvement enhances the learning process. They will absorb an enormous amount of learning from an active training session, far more than from studying company policy manuals, technical manuals, and three-ring binders stuffed with "how-to" bulletins. If you want adults to learn, keep them active. Don't use third-grade methods to teach a group of adults. It won't work.

Participation is also essential to the adult learning process. It generates mental activity and analytical thinking. The use of case studies creates involvement and can develop both analytical skills and decision-making skills. Role play situations develop organizational, communications, questioning, and persuasive skills. They also provide verbal feedback on understanding of the material being taught.

Programmed learning materials generate student participation. They develop the thinking process and provide immediate motivational reinforcement to the learner. Buzz sessions or group discussions provide an opportunity for problem-solving and the development of decision-making skills on a group basis. They also provide for an exercise in group dynamics and group leadership.

In all probability, however, the majority of your training efforts will be on the job, especially in the development of required skills. Don't throw the employee to the wolves, put him on the job, and expect all the learning to take place by osmosis and observation. Training efforts must be planned carefully and executed with patience if the desired results are to be obtained. Never overlook the significance of relevancy, activity, and participation in the adult learning process. When all three are present, learning will take place.

The Five-Step Method of Teaching

Those of you who were around in 1941 can remember the enormous task this nation faced in an immediate mobilization for World War II. The one factor we did not have was time. It had to be done immediately. Industry had to make a rapid transition from the manufacture of peacetime goods to the weapons of war. Millions of Americans had to be trained, almost overnight, to man the production lines. Millions of men and women had to learn jobs they had never performed. More millions of military personnel had to be trained to implement the tools of war.

In facing such an unbelievable task of training people, it seems ironic that it would take a world war to return us to a simple and basic way of achieving it. There was no time for philosophy or theory; it was a matter of getting right down to basics. Thus, the five-step method of training was born. It is still recognized as the best method of training another person to do a job.

Today's manager would do well to get back on the track of basics in training subordinates, whether teaching a new task or giving remedial training for corrective purposes. The basics work. As you use the five-step method of teaching, it is important that every step be used in every case. Don't skip a single step.

1. *Tell* the employee what and why you are going to teach. Establish the relevancy. If the employee understands why a task is important and where it fits into the overall operation, he is more likely to learn it. We tend to learn those things we see as important more thoroughly. Adults learn well only when the relevancy of the training is recognized.

2. *Show* the employee how to do it, step by step, explaining each step as you do it. Move slowly, because not all of us learn at the same pace. Be patient. Don't fall into the old trap of rushing through the task, standing back, and saying, "There, see how easy it is?" Things are easy when you understand them. But the employee doesn't have that understanding yet. Move slowly.

3. *Watch* the employee perform the task, one step at a time, to be certain each part was thoroughly learned. This is your opportunity for real communication, to see whether the teacher taught and the learner learned. If correction is needed, now is the time to do it, explaining why and how.

4. This step is really an extension of step 3, but it is vital to understanding. As the employee performs the task (step 3), have him *explain verbally* what is being done and why, step by step. This gives you not only a visual observation of performance, but a verbal confirmation of understanding as well. Misconceptions can

be cleared up immediately. You will also get a feel for the importance the employee places on the task.

5. *Check back* on the employee periodically, for two very important reasons: The first is to be certain the employee continues to perform the right way. Skills deteriorate. We forget. We misunderstand. Check back to avoid "slippage." The second reason is to give the employee important positive feedback. We all need to feel a sense of achievement. This is your chance to foster the motivation for continued performance.

There's nothing earthshaking in these five important steps. They are quite basic. Nevertheless, they are regularly overlooked or ignored by supervisors. Managers feel they are too elementary. But if they can successfully mobilize the greatest nation on earth, what can they do in your area of company responsibility?

Two very important parts of teaching are patience and feedback. They are basic to any good teacher and to any good manager. Even when an employee doesn't grasp things right away and reteaching is necessary, remember—patience and feedback.

Determining Training Needs

Billions of dollars are wasted in this country every year teaching people to do things they already know how to do. Seems ridiculous, doesn't it? Yet it is true. Managers train people because they think training will solve their problems. Training will solve problems only when lack of skills or knowledge *is* the problem. Too few managers have learned to recognize the difference between an employee who doesn't know how to do something (a discrepancy in knowledge) and an employee who knows how, but isn't doing it right (a discrepancy in execution).

In the second instance, it isn't a training problem. It is a management problem. There is a big difference between "can do" and "will do," and unless you learn to recognize the difference, you will be wasting enormous amounts of time and money in training people to do something they already know how to do, and they still won't do it.

Naturally, in determining training needs, you will have two groups to consider, new employees and present employees. The required job skills should be the same for each, perhaps with differences in proficiency levels. That is, experienced employees should have reached a level of skill that more nearly approximates full mastery of the job. New employees will have a larger performance gap to close. Both groups, however, should be striving for the same level of proficiency—a zero performance gap. Your first step is to identify the performance gap so you can plan the training necessary to close it.

The starting point is a thorough analysis of the job description. The job description is a list of the employee's responsibilities. So the logical question for you to answer is, "What does the employee need in the way of skills and knowledge in order to do this job properly?" Be sure to limit your list to essentials, avoiding the "nice to know" things. Stick to the basic skills and knowledge that are absolutely required in order to perform satisfactorily. The peripheral information can be learned later.

The next step is to observe the job being performed by a present employee. You will certainly see several essential skills that were not in the job description. Observe—don't guess or speculate. It is also wise to ask the present employee to list all the required skills. The list will be another valuable input to help you determine training needs.

Another valuable source is your own experience. You are familiar with the job to a large degree. But don't allow this familiarity to be the only source; that happens all too often. Let me stress again: "None of us is as smart as all of us." Use all resources when determining training needs.

Determining training needs for present employees may take a little more effort on your part. Actually there are two primary areas of training of concern: training to improve performance on the present job and training to prepare the employee to move up to greater jobs. Both should definitely be planned for all employees.

It must be recognized, however, that excellence in the present job is the first prerequisite for promotion, or it should be. Grooming an employee for a more responsible job has a definite positive effect on the employee's attitude toward present performance. At this point, however, let's turn our attention toward improving performance in the present job.

To repeat, there is a difference between "can do" and "will do." If the employee knows how to do the job but simply isn't doing it right, don't waste time and effort in trying to train for correction. There is a reason the employee isn't performing properly, and that reason must be determined and then removed or corrected. That is a management activity other than training. Don't let yourself get caught in this familiar trap.

Distinguishing between "can do" and "will do" problems is not as difficult as it may seem. It requires asking a very logical sequence of questions, but you must be absolutely objective and honest in answering each of them. Some of the questions must be posed directly to the employee, but most can be answered by you, the manager. Follow this sequence of questioning:

1. Has the employee *ever* done the job correctly?
2. Has the employee been taught to do it correctly?
3. If you were to offer a $1 million tax-free cash bonus on the spot to the employee to do the job correctly, could he do it?

If the answer to any of the above questions is "no," you have a training problem. Start planning to teach the employee. If the answer to question 1 or 2 is "yes," there are some further questions to be posed:

How long ago was the employee trained?

Has the employee forgotten?

Have interim job assignments taken the employee away from the skill involved?

Has the employee become disenchanted with the job in question and lost interest because of other assignments that proved to be more interesting?

How often does the employee actually use the skill? Does he have enough practice?

Does the employee place enough value on proper performance?
Is it rewarding enough in his mind?
Are peer pressures causing the employee to perform unsat-
isfactorily?
Is it easier (in his mind) or more enjoyable to do it his way?
Is it worth the time and effort to change him?

Following this line of questioning will help you determine
whether you are facing a training problem or a management problem. If, under any circumstances whatsoever, the employee *could*
do the job correctly, forget training. You had better take a hard,
objective look at the way the employee is being managed, the way
the employee's job is organized, or the potential effect of peer
pressure. Something other than inability is causing your problem
and training won't solve it.

Let's assume that your investigation has proven that the employee is incapable of performing properly under any circumstances. You do have a training problem. Where do we go from here?

The first step is to isolate the things that need to be taught.
Separate the things the employee knows from those he does not
know. To do this, you must have the employee demonstrate the
skills he is presently using. There will surely be parts of the job
being done properly. If the employee doesn't do anything right,
you may have a few flaws in your hiring procedure. Physically
demonstrated skills, with close observation by you, are the best
means of separating ability from inability. Plan your training
around the inabilities only.

Every job requires not only skills, but also some knowledge.
Examples are the ability to read blueprints, to use a dictionary, to
use reference manuals, catalogs, and price sheets, to use certain
specifications, to do arithmetic, and to understand grammar. This
list could be endless. Obviously skills and knowledge overlap in
certain areas, such as using reference manuals and specification
sheets. But the employee must be tested to determine what is
missing in essential knowledge. The testing could be verbal or
written. You may already have a battery of employment tests that

are used to measure knowledge. Use every resource available in testing the employee. Determine where your emphasis is to be placed in training. Identify the performance gap.

Planning for Training

Once you have determined what must be included in the training, the next step is to write the instructional objectives. Don't rely on divine guidance or seat-of-the-pants intuition. The instructional objective must contain the answers to three vital questions:

1. What will the learner be able to do after the training?
2. What are the conditions or restrictions under which the employee will be required to do it for you (the demonstration)?
3. What are the minimum standards you will accept (performance standard)?

As you answer the first question, use terms that describe observable behavior; for example, build, calculate, recite, complete, ride, operate, differentiate, type, drive, lift, separate, dismantle, reassemble, join, repair, replace, or locate. These are all observable, demonstrable behaviors.

After the training is completed, the demonstration must be conducted under certain restrictive conditions. What tools will the employee be allowed to use? What will be withheld? You may allow the use of references (manuals), certain tools and equipment, a calculator, or a stepladder. Certain items may not be allowed. For example, if you are testing for a basic knowledge of arithmetic, you may require that all computations be made by hand, using only pencil and paper. An electronic calculator may not be allowed.

The third question establishes the performance standard for the demonstration. It states what performance you, the manager, would accept as satisfactory, would consider "passing the test." Included in the performance standard would be such criteria as how many, how few, how fast, how completely, how accurately, and what margin of error is allowable.

Here are some examples of instructional objectives that contain the essential elements:

1. Given the cost of a piece of merchandise, the employee will be able, with the help of an electronic calculator, to compute proper sales prices based on a markup of 20 percent, or a 20 percent margin of gross profit, without error.

2. Given the standard set of hand tools and analytic equipment, the employee will be able to locate and correct no less than five of the six malfunctions rigged into a standard automobile engine, and do so within 30 minutes.

3. Given the standard reference manuals and an electronic calculator, the employee will be able to calculate the most favorable purchase price on twenty SKUs, with at least 90 percent accuracy.

Instructional objectives aren't really difficult to write, so long as you know the behavioral outcome you want. In writing the objective, you are really only answering one question in the employee's mind, "How are you going to know if I learned it?"

Here is an extremely important point. Before you begin to teach, give the employee the instructional objective in writing. Let the employee know at the outset what he is going to be expected to demonstrate after the training unit is finished. If the employee knows precisely what he is expected to learn, there is relevancy to the training. Unless the employee sees and understands the relevancy, he has no reason or desire to learn it. A clearly stated instructional objective also keeps you on the right track, and helps you avoid peripheral "nice-to-know" information that isn't relevant to the demonstration.

Don't take the lazy way out either. Many managers find it easy to give the employee a book or manual that describes the work skills and expect the employee to learn the skills. It won't work. No child ever learned to ride a bicycle by reading a book. A golf pro doesn't care whether you can describe the proper stance or grip of the club, or recite the history of the game. That pro only wants to know whether you can swat the ball the right distance, in the right direction, with the right consistency. Take the same approach in your training efforts. Concentrate on teaching an employee to do the right thing. If you can't see it or measure it, don't bother teaching it. If you are teaching something that cannot be measured, you may have trouble in proving that you are teaching anything at all.

Evaluation of Supervisory Practices (ESP Rating)

1. Do I accept the responsibility for training my employees as completely my responsibility?
2. Do I consider training as a continuous and ongoing activity?
3. Am I patient enough with employees who do not learn as rapidly as others?
4. Do I religiously use the five-step method of training, without skipping any of the steps?
5. Do I specifically and accurately identify each employee's performance gap in determining targets for training?
6. Do I clearly establish relevancy at the outset of each training unit?
7. Do I use active, participative training methods?
8. Do I clearly differentiate between discrepancies in knowledge and discrepancies in execution before planning for training?
9. Do I provide training to help employees reach for greater responsibilities?
10. Prior to each training unit, do I prepare written instructional objectives and give the employee a copy?

7 | Coaching and Counseling

Coaching employees on the job is a never-ending process. Skills begin slipping, employees forget, the routine aspects of the job take their toll. There are many reasons employees will begin to slip away from the basic skills that made them productive. When slippage occurs, corrective measures must be taken. Coaching could be considered an extension of training, or a continuous training effort. Nevertheless, there will always be a need for some coaching. Coaching is an effective means of changing a productive employee into a highly productive employee. It deals with the furthering of skills and knowledge required on the job.

Counseling, on the other hand, has a more personal aspect to it. Counseling is a one-on-one situation in which you sit down with an employee—in private—and discuss problems that have a bearing on his job performance. Something could be worrying the employee—domestic problems, morale problems, attitude problems, health problems, disciplinary problems, or grievances could be bothering him. Whatever the cause, the symptoms tell you something is interfering with job performance. It must be discovered and corrected, if possible.

But counseling isn't necessarily negative. Perhaps an employee wants to discuss his future with the company, and start a self-development program. The employee is seeking your advice. You may call an employee in for the very same reason.

The Coaching Session

Coaching employees is a one-on-one situation, a fact overlooked by some managers. Granted, certain employee behaviors can be changed by holding group meetings, but group training sessions are often held when the specific behaviors that need to be altered are individual or isolated. Naturally, a manager wants to develop teamwork within the work group, but individual coaching is often the only answer.

Individual performance causes group performance. That is, if each individual succeeds (primary objective) the group has to succeed (secondary objective). It's automatic. Great professional football teams win the Super Bowl only because each individual on the team succeeds at his own assignment—consistently. As a result of this individual professionalism, there is a group victory. Teamwork is important, but don't rely solely on group training. Training, coaching, and managing individuals cause the group to succeed.

Just as with any training situation, you must be able to identify the behavior you are trying to achieve. What behavior have you observed that needs changing? What is the specific difference between the behavior you observe and the behavior you want? If you don't know what you're after and what it should look like, don't waste your time "coaching in the clouds." Be specific, absolutely specific, in what you expect. Write an instructional objective for it, following the procedure given in Chapter 6. If you can't write an instructional objective, you're already off base.

Let's assume that you have identified the behavior you want changed. How do you change it? You aren't going to be very successful if you proceed as many managers have: "Come on, Linda, that's not the way you were taught to do that. Get with it!" Or

"Ken, I've shown you twice how to do that. Now do it the way I showed you—or your replacement will." This isn't coaching, and it's unlikely to produce any more than mediocre results. Coaching is teaching, not scolding.

Here is a logical step-by-step procedure for planning and conducting a coaching session:

1. Observe the present behavior, compare it with desired behavior, and identify what needs to be changed. Identify the performance gap.

2. Discuss the deviation with the employee. Is the employee aware that his behavior is wrong? Is the employee able to differentiate between present behavior and expected behavior? What are the employee's reasons for incorrect behavior? Do they seem justifiable (to him)?

3. Be patient and understanding as you ask a few pertinent questions:

"How can we improve your skills?"

"How can I help you?"

"Is there a better way of doing this?"

"How can we speed up your production?"

"How can we make this job easier or faster?"

Getting the employee to talk about the performance will serve a valuable purpose. It gives the employee some insight into the job and improves his perspective on the importance of the job. It also shows that you are genuinely interested in him.

4. Use the five-step method presented in Chapter 6 to demonstrate the desired performance until the employee can do it correctly and can explain the reason for doing it that way.

5. When the employee has demonstrated the proper performance, let him know you are pleased with what you see and that you expect to see it continue. Don't do this in a threatening manner, or it may undo everything you have accomplished. You want productivity and growth, not mere obedience.

Few managers spend the necessary time to observe their employees' behavior. They often get enmeshed in the "administrivia" of the job—paperwork, reports, handling complaints—and fail to plan the time for on-the-job coaching for each employee. On the other hand, don't "bird-dog" employees to see what they are doing.

Take the time on a regular basis to be with each employee right on the job, discussing the job, discussing company plans, discussing the weather, family, or World Series. Doing so provides the opportunity to observe performance and plan for needed coaching. It also has some motivational value. It shows that you place a lot of importance on both the job and the employees.

Spending time with employees may be more difficult for some managers, but it must be done on a regular basis. Sales managers, for example, must go on the road with sales personnel, but it's a valuable activity for many reasons. Coaching of sales representatives, as of all employees, is a never-ending process.

For some reason, many sales managers have a problem during the first, or observation, phase of coaching. They find it difficult merely to observe a sales representative during a sales call, and stay out of it. If the salesperson gets into trouble, the manager can't resist jumping in to salvage the sale. This is terribly destructive to a sales representative, and should be avoided, even at the cost of one lost sale. The primary objective is to strengthen the sales representative; that particular sale is secondary. The sales manager is there to observe and learn. As long as he is talking, he isn't learning a thing.

The coaching is to be done after the call, not during it. Let the sales representative discuss the call. What went wrong? What went well? How could I have handled the questions better? How do I need to change my approach? The salesperson needs this analysis and insight to plan for the next call.

If the sales manager wishes to give a demonstration, there are two ways of doing it. Take the sales representative to the motel room and do some role playing, or accompany the sales representative on a sales call, and carry the ball all the way. The sales representative will observe. If the latter method is used, it should not be done with one of the salesman's regular customers. It could damage the salesman's credibility with the customer.

Regardless of the type of work group you supervise, it should be one of your personal objectives to budget your time to observe each employee's performance on a regular basis, and then do it. It will pay off, both for you and for your employees.

A good manager coaches his employees in much the same way a good basketball or football coach coaches a team. Corrective measures are based on observable behavior that needs to be changed or improved. Coaching, just as in sports, may be an immediate means of altering direction that needs to be altered. Through coaching at half-time the entire strategy of a football game can be changed in order to cope with the strategy of the opposing team.

Time and again, I have seen competitive conditions dictate immediate changes in marketing strategy. I recall one case in particular, when our company's intelligence sources advised us of a competitor's intentions of mounting a massive campaign to introduce a new product in the southern states. We geared up to meet the offense with intensive advertising and promotional campaigns and a special coaching program to get our sales personnel ready for some "one-upmanship." Advertising campaigns were quickly developed, media were contacted, promotional efforts were developed, and the sales force was readied for its part in meeting the onslaught.

You guessed it. Our intelligence source had been misinformed. The assault was to be launched in one month in the Pacific Northwest, one of our weakest markets. You never saw such coaching sessions in your life. We even flew first-class to Seattle to get there thirty-eight feet sooner. We had scores of people to coach in a matter of days. Sales personnel were called into a special meeting to learn new presentation methods that would offset the competitive efforts. Local media representatives were called in to take over the already designed advertising campaign. Promotional material arrived on time and was delivered immediately to all retail outlets. We were lucky! We launched our campaign exactly one week prior to our competitor's campaign and successfully neutralized its efforts.

Most coaching efforts, however, are simply in the day-to-day activities of the job, concentrating on the skills that need improving or need to be taught. A manager must accept this ongoing activity as a way of life. The fact that an employee has learned certain skills does not necessarily mean he will continue to perform properly.

There are many reasons skills deteriorate. One of the most common is a phenomenon called "professional degeneration," and it happens in every profession in the world. In most cases, it is caused by the routineness of the job, the repetitive activities. The employee begins tiring of the routine and starts to change things just to provide some job variety. After a series of changes, the employee frequently finds that he has strayed a long way from the basic fundamentals that made him productive in the first place. Effective and regular coaching is one of the best means of getting the employee back on the right track and of preventing deviation before the basic productivity is lost.

Another reason we see employee behavior change is a sense of independence. Employees often want to do their own thing, to experiment, to try things their way. This is not necessarily bad. Employees frequently bring fresh thinking and innovative approaches to a job. The astute manager will recognize this and allow some free rein in experimentation. At the same time, the situation should be monitored carefully to avoid excessive damage. Freedom to experiment is the embryo of innovation, a fact well recognized by progressive managers.

The Counseling Session

As opposed to coaching, counseling has a different connotation. It may involve advice, opinions, or consultation. It is aimed toward directing the judgment or the conduct of the employee. It could be a disciplinary confrontation, or the employee may wish to voice a grievance. It could be that the employee needs to discuss a personal problem or "blow off some steam." Whatever the reason, the manager must be available.

You will encounter two kinds of counseling sessions—the session you call and the session requested by the employee. Neither is more important than the other. Both are important to you and to the employee.

Your reason for calling a counseling session may be something you heard or observed that told you things weren't going right for the employee. Perhaps morale seems to have dipped. Perhaps the employee has become a "loner," avoids other employees, and has become belligerent and argumentative. Perhaps he has become indifferent about the job, doesn't seem up to par, shows no particular ambition, ignores safety regulations, leaves work undone.

Whatever the reason, something has to be done about it. You feel a need to call the employee in and talk about it. Again, a step-by-step procedure will make it more productive and less painful for both you and the employee:

1. Try to determine why the employee is displaying the wrong behavior. Talking with other employees may give you some insight. Observing the employee concerned on a frequent basis may help provide the answer. Don't settle for treating the symptoms; determine the cause and go after it. You may or may not learn much about the problem, but it's certainly an important first step.

2. Plan ahead for the counseling session. Your plan should include the answers to these questions:

"What have I heard that justifies calling the employee in?"
"What do I think might be the cause?"
"What effect is it having on productivity?"
"What effect is it having on others?"
"What do I plan to say to the employee?"
"How will I get the employee to talk about this?"
"How will I help the employee save face, so I get positive results?"
"What will I suggest?"

3. After you have planned your counseling session, notify the employee a day or so in advance of the meeting. Tell the employee you wish to have a discussion about his work. This will give the employee a day or so to think about his on-the-job performance, to conduct a little self-analysis, and to gain some insight on his individual performance. Never call a counseling session on the spur of the moment unless an emergency, hazardous, or extremely urgent disciplinary situation exists—for example, a flagrant violation of safety procedures that could endanger the employee or others.

4. Set the stage for the meeting. Keep the meeting private, with absolutely no interruptions. Stop the phone calls and lock the door. If this isn't possible, hold the meeting away from your office. Once the employee opens up and starts discussing the problem, an interruption can be disastrous.

5. Put the employee at ease with some small talk, perhaps a cup of coffee. Unless this is a disciplinary situation, you will want to ease into it gently. Discuss some of the positive aspects of the job before moving to the negatives. Some typical questions might be:

"How is the job coming?"
"Where are you doing the best?"
"How are you progressing?"
"Anywhere you need help?"
"Any particular problems?"

These questions will certainly get the discussion started, but don't spend all day on them.

6. Get to the point of the meeting:

"John, I think there's something on your mind that's having some effect on your work. Can you tell me what it is?"

"Marie, you have always done a satisfactory job, but lately I've noticed something seems to be bothering you. Any idea what it is?"

"Bill, several employees have noticed that you seem to be dragging your feet lately. What's the problem?"

7. Listen, listen, listen! Encourage the employee to discuss the situation by using these nudges: "Uh huh," "Oh?" "How's that?" or a simple nod. It is important that the employee analyze the situation and ventilate any feelings he may have about it.

8. Help the employee save face, or your recommended solution may go unheeded. Let the employee know that you or others have faced similar situations, that he is not alone. Once in a while merely saying "I understand" or "I see" will help. Your objective is to improve, not blame.

9. Come to an agreement as to what needs to be done to avoid further loss in productivity. Discuss specific behaviors you find detrimental, and what is to be done about it.

10. Set a date to discuss the employee's improvement.

11. Make a written note of your discussion, including date, time, location, subject discussed, and recommendations made. File this note for future reference, in case more severe disciplinary measures become necessary.

When you call the counseling session, you have the advantage of planning ahead for it. But when an employee asks to talk to you, it's a different story. It usually starts something like this, "Mr. Collins, when could I have about 30 minutes to talk to you about something?" Or the employee may barge right into your office and say, "Mrs. Allen, I need to talk to you."

Unless it is an emergency situation, *don't* jump into a counseling session immediately. Set a time lapse before the meeting, if possible. Try something like this: "How about 8 o'clock in the morning, Joe? OK?" "By the way, Joe, to be sure I set aside enough time, what was it you wanted to discuss?" If these questions uncover the topic of the discussion, you will have gained some valuable time for planning your part of the discussion. You will be in a much better position to help the employee.

The basic ground rules for conducting this meeting are about the same as previously outlined, with a few significant differences:

1. You may be no more than a sounding board to let an employee air a problem, probably a personal problem.

2. Don't try to play God, priest, or psychologist. You aren't qualified. Giving advice on personal problems is dangerous and can backfire right in your face. Just hear the employee out. If it is a problem of finances, you might refer the employee to a financial counselor. You might wish to refer the employee to a marriage counselor or a minister, depending on the nature of the problem. But don't try to solve personal problems yourself. It's dangerous.

3. If it is a personal problem, it's none of your darn business, unless it is affecting the employee's performance on the job. If it is, it is very much your business.

4. After the employee has vented the problem, always ask, "What do you feel can be done about it?" Get the employee to recommend a solution, if possible.

5. End the discussion by thanking the employee for coming to you, and ask if he would like to get together again in a week or so to see what has changed.

6. What the two of you discuss is confidential. Keep it that way!

Managers often avoid counseling sessions until a real crisis occurs. This is unfortunate because counseling used on a regular basis can be very motivational. Professional managers make it a habit to counsel their employees on a regular basis, simply to discuss the job and to give the employee an opportunity to open up and discuss anything on his mind. It lets the employee know the manager is interested in him, listens to him, is aware of his contribution, and respects him. Employees frequently have many things on their minds they would like to discuss if given an opportunity. Perhaps none of these is of a negative nature, but the employee needs to talk about them. It may be that an employee just wants to express to the manager how completely delighted he is with the job and the company.

I recall an interesting example a few years ago. I was on a flight to Atlanta, Georgia, playing gin rummy with my supervisor, when he said, "Jim, I've never seen an employee who seemed so happy in his job. What is it that makes you feel this way?" Believe me, I wasn't completely happy, and there were a few things I really wanted to discuss, some negative and some positive. But he knew how to open the conversation so that I felt completely free to discuss anything. The conversation lasted over an hour, including things I loved about my work and things that could be improved. He said very little and listened intently. He was learning and I was feeling better every minute. Frankly, the open conversation was extremely motivational for me and informative for him. He was a good manager, and still is.

I was actually discussing things I should and could be doing to produce greater results. He was letting me increase my own workload and assume greater responsibility. I was setting objectives for myself that needed to be achieved—and he let me.

But the most important factor was, this man was professional enough to realize that employees need to talk about their jobs. Your employees need to talk about their jobs. Offer them the opportunity regularly. Employees need to talk about the negative and positive aspects of their jobs. They need to ventilate. They need to talk about their successes in the job, their satisfaction with their managers. We all need this. After we have done it, we return to the work situation with a renewed feeling of energy. It is therapeutic!

Evaluation of Supervisory Practices (ESP Rating)

1. Do I plan and use regular and frequent coaching sessions to further my employees' skills?
2. Prior to coaching an employee, do I specifically identify the behavior I wish to change?
3. Do I take the time, on a regular basis, to observe behavior so that I can identify skills that might be slipping?
4. Am I a good listener during counseling sessions?
5. Do I avoid giving advice regarding personal or domestic problems?
6. Do I get employees to recommend solutions to their own problems?

7. Do I periodically call a counseling session to discuss an employee's in-job growth and future?
8. Do I avoid calling spur-of-the-moment counseling sessions for disciplinary purposes?
9. Do I keep *all* counseling sessions absolutely private and confidential?
10. Do I keep written records of discussions held during coaching and counseling sessions for further reference?

8 | Performance Feedback

Perhaps the most important question in the industrial and professional world, yet the most unasked and unanswered, is, "How am I doing?" Employees want—and need—to know how well they are doing, how well they are satisfying their managers, and how their performance compares with expected performance.

There is nothing in the world like doing a good job and being told you have done a good job. It serves as a mainspring for further achievement. It builds teamwork, it promotes high quality, it generates a desire to "go that extra mile," and it develops a sense of pride in what you are doing. All of these results show up directly on the bottom line of the operating statement.

Why, then, don't we see more of it in supervisor/subordinate relationships? Basically, because we assume too much! We assume that an employee knows exactly what is expected of him. We assume that he knows when work is deviating from the expected norms. We assume the employee knows how well he is doing. The employee assumes that the job is being performed to the manager's satisfaction.

Too frequently we assume that clear-cut communication has taken place between supervisor and subordinate, yet we constantly hear comments like these around the job:

"That's not the way you're supposed to do it!"
"Why didn't you tell me?"
"If I had only known. . . ."
"Can't you get it straight?"
"I told you how easy it was."
"What's wrong with you?"
"I guess I misunderstood."
"I wish he'd let me know."
"You're supposed to know what you're doing."
"I thought you had experience."
"You've been around here long enough to know."
"Oh! That's what you want!"

These are all indicators that something is going wrong, and company productivity is going to suffer as a result. It may even put an employee's job in jeopardy. Most of these situations are caused by failing to give employees regular, clear, complete, and positive feedback regarding exactly what they are expected to do (and how well), and how they are performing against that standard.

Before you jump to any defensive conclusions, think about this: Research proves that most employees *don't* know exactly what the manager expects in the way of job performance; they don't know exactly what it takes to please the manager; and they don't know exactly how well they are performing in the opinion of the manager. Further research shows the problem is compounded: Most managers are convinced that these things aren't true for their particular work group.

Almost every employee (yourself included) sincerely wants to do a good job for his boss. You can help the employee by providing plenty of feedback, so the employee knows at all times how well he is performing. Too many supervisors make the mistake of withholding feedback (the "no news is good news" syndrome) until something goes wrong. Then all hell breaks loose, tempers flare, feelings are hurt, and employee productivity is lost. There's no need for this waste. Make it a habit regularly to sit down with each of your employees and discuss the requirements of the job.

Do the performance standards of the job clearly state in written form what is considered satisfactory performance? Was a copy of the standards given to the employee? Or are they buried, by some ridiculous company policy, in a three-ring binder in the personnel office? Denying an employee a copy of the standards against which his performance will be measured is nothing short of criminal and immoral.

Are your standards of performance for your employees realistic? Do they promote mediocrity—or excellence? If *your* boss walked up to you right now and asked how you would rate the performance of the group working for you, how would you answer? Before reading farther, please close the book for a few moments and decide how you would answer that question. (Come on, do it!)

Consider the answer you would have given. What would you have said? Would you have said that they're OK, they get the job done, I'm satisfied with their performance, or I've got a good bunch here? If your answer ran along these veins, you have a problem. There is absolutely nothing in these replies that indicates anything more than average or satisfactory job performance. There is no indication of excellence or high performance.

Are you merely "satisfied" or "happy" with their performance? Oh, sure, they're getting the job done and getting the work out. But is it on a day-to-day basis, routine, doing it the same way, keeping up with the workload? Or is your group stretching, constantly improving in quality and quantity, finding better ways to get the job done? If the latter is not the case, perhaps you should take a hard look at your management efforts.

When was the last time one of your employees came to you and asked to be given more responsibility? When was the last time an employee suggested a better way to get the job done? When was the last time an employee asked you for suggestions on how he could do a better job? Unless these happened lately, there is something wrong in the relationship between you and your people.

Frankly, many managers have to answer "never." If that is the case, you should ask yourself why. Do your employees feel free to come to you with such questions? Do they feel free, or do you just think they feel free?

A really effective manager makes it a habit to sit down with each employee and discuss the employee's job. Note the word "discuss." It is a two-way communication in which you and the employee both discuss the job. Any employee (yourself included) really wants and deserves to know how well he is performing, what's being done well, how it can be done better, and how the job itself can be improved. It's just good management.

These discussions, held on a regular basis, keep the lines of communication open between you and your employees. They help maintain a high level of morale. Unfortunately the majority of managers abdicate this one-on-one discussion, except in disciplinary or corrective situations. But the discussion can be the healthiest therapy a manager can apply. It shows that you have a genuine concern for your employees, that you listen to them, that you want to help them grow in their jobs. It can be one of the greatest motivating factors you can apply.

Why not start next Monday, making it one of your primary objectives to discuss each employee's job on a regular basis? Don't look at it as a "corrective" measure at all, rather as a "motivational" effort. You will be surprised at the results, and you will soon find each of your employees looking forward to the discussions. You will find them voluntarily coming to you with suggestions for greater job output. They will do it because they know you care about them.

To make the first such discussion most effective, to make it easier for both you and the employee, and to get it started off on a positive note, here are a couple of suggestions:

1. Make it a point not to discuss any negative (corrective) items, unless the employee brings one up voluntarily.

2. Limit your questions to the following:

"What part of your job do you really like most?" "Why?"
"How do you feel we could improve the job (not the performance)?"

"Are there any additional things you would like to be doing?"
"Is there anything in your present job where you feel I could
help you strengthen your work?"
"Do you have any suggestions about where I could be of more
help to you?"
"Are there any other supervisors who could give you any specific help you would like to have?"

Granted, the first such discussion may leave an employee in a
mild state of bewilderment. But as soon as your employees recognize that you are serious about the discussions, that you really are
concerned, that you listen, that you give the help they ask for, you
will have laid some important groundwork for a strong, productive
manager/employee relationship.

Feedback consists of more than "Here's what's expected, and
here's what you're doing." An important part of feedback to an
employee is the giving of yourself, your time, your help. Your
interest and concern are extremely important to all employees.
Every employee needs them on a regular and continuing basis.

Managers often feel that the only feedback the employee really
needs takes place in the annual or semiannual performance appraisal. Under this kind of philosophy, the performance appraisal,
if held, often turns out to be no more than a traumatic confrontation that jars the very foundation of an employee's emotional security. The employee usually looks forward to the appraisal as
much as he would to root canal work.

Performance appraisal, much like training, is not a once-in-a-
while situation. It's an ongoing activity. Performance appraisal *is*
feedback to the employee. Some kind of appraisal should take
place every time a manager and an employee come together. It
may take no more than 30 seconds at times. But the constant feed-
ing back to the employee of information is needed to sustain in-
job growth.

The big annual or semiannual performance appraisal is an important part of feedback, but it doesn't need to be a traumatic
confrontation. If it is planned and conducted properly, employees

will look forward to it with eagerness. It's an opportunity for them to receive some well-deserved recognition and to do some effective planning for ways to gain still more recognition.

If you, the manager, have established clear-cut job descriptions and performance standards, and have provided the help your employees need to learn and to grow, the performance appraisal can be a productive and delightful experience for both of you. It is the culmination of all the mini appraisals you have held with employees for months. It is the launching pad for the period ahead. An entire book could easily be devoted to performance appraisals alone, and many excellent ones have been.

Most feedback, however, takes place in the day-to-day contact with employees, keeping them constantly informed as to their performance. Your contact with the employee should contain four essential elements: (1) Here's what is expected. (2) Here's what you are doing well. (3) Here's where you need help. (4) Here's what we are doing about it.

Performance appraisals often turn into complete disasters because the discussion turns to personality traits rather than job performance. There are, of course, some logical reasons for this. Managers tend to mold their employees after themselves. They want employees to act like them, to think like them, and to display similar personality traits.

This is especially true for managers who have a very favorable self-image. They want employees to emulate them, thinking this will improve productivity. Such managers often find they are doing no more than training actors, rather than developing productive workers. Unless an undesirable personality trait is having a measurable, adverse effect on job performance, it should not be discussed during the appraisal.

The hiring procedure, too, often promotes personality discussions. When interviewing applicants, we seek certain personality characteristics such as friendliness, cooperativeness, aggressiveness, extroversion, and warmth. Since we are looking for such characteristics, it's only natural to feel that we should measure them. Therefore, they frequently become prime targets in the performance appraisal.

Some companies have even gone so far as assigning numerical values to each of the characteristics, making it easier for a manager to "score" each employee. Even a practicing psychologist would find it difficult to determine weighted values for personality characteristics, yet managers do it with ease. Unfortunately, these subjective judgments are often used to determine employee salaries, increases, promotions, and job grade levels.

Granted, personality is important in many jobs. For instance, a salesman with a personality that antagonizes customers would be extremely counterproductive. Nearly every job that requires public contact demands certain positive characteristics, jobs such as receptionists, secretaries, sales clerks, bank tellers, and customer service personnel. If certain characteristics are important to you, find them at the interview table. Don't try to change personalities on the job. Your time would be better spent on other management activities.

No one will deny that personality characteristics have a bearing on the way a man does his work; they are often the tools with which he does his work. But, as far as evaluating his accomplishments is concerned, there is very little correlation between "results achieved" and the fact that he is trustworthy, loyal, helpful, friendly, courteous, kind, obedient, cheerful, thrifty, brave, clean, and reverent. The cold, hard truth of the matter is that if the man produces the desired results, gets the job done, and meets his objectives, whether or not he is brave is purely academic. If the man does not meet his objectives, a retrospective analysis may reveal that certain character weaknesses have contributed to his failure. Weaknesses then become targets for improvement.

Obviously, evaluation of results is primary, and any further evaluation is immaterial unless the results are unsatisfactory. In such cases, analysis will almost invariably reveal that results were poor because of failure to perform certain key tasks. The reason for failure to perform could be lack of knowledge of the job, lack of proper motivation, lack of proper supervision, other functions taking precedence, or lack of initiative or responsibility on the part of the employee.

The principal point up to now is that the performance appraisal, to be effective, must direct its efforts toward accomplishment, the results achieved as measured against the standards set. If, and only if, the desired results were not achieved should we look toward personal qualities to see if they contributed to the failure to reach objectives and decide whether corrective action is possible.

Such personal characteristics as initiative, judgment, adaptability, poise, integrity, emotional stability, self-confidence, and versatility would fall under this retrospective analysis. These must be considered (since they are causal agents), but only a psychologist is capable of measuring them. A quick review of dozens of ineffective performance appraisal systems will reveal such items being used as criteria for judging an employee's performance. These are *not* the correct targets for appraisal or for employee feedback.

A Word About Criticism

It has often been argued that there is no such thing as constructive criticism, that it always destroys something in a person. If this is true, it is because of the insensitive way in which the criticism is delivered. No one likes to be told he is doing things wrong, but no one resents being shown a way to improve.

Think how often we have seen and heard criticism delivered in a destructive manner:

"I'm the boss, and I want it done my way."
"Don't argue, just do it."
"I'm doing this for your own good."
"This hurts me more than it hurts you."
"If you don't do it, your replacement will."
"I don't have time to explain it, just do it."
"Here's what you're doing wrong."

And the worst is the manager who delivers criticism in front of others. This approach to criticism shows no sensitivity toward the feelings of others. What the manager destroys (psychologically) is greater than what he might correct. Any sensitive supervisor realizes that the very purpose of criticism is to help an employee improve, to improve productivity, to improve attitudes, and at the same time to protect the employee's morale, self-confidence, self-image, and enthusiasm.

Many managers avoid direct criticism altogether. They have a basic drive to be a "good guy" and don't want to disrupt that great relationship. The relationship won't be damaged in the least through sensitive, constructive help. If anything, the relationship can be strengthened, especially if the employee feels he has been helped.

But no matter how sensitive or tactful you may be, some people resent criticism of any kind. You must lay aside your personal feelings, bite the bullet, and point out the employee's shortcomings and what you expect changed. You owe this feedback to your employee, and it is essential to the employee's growth and development. It is also essential to the health of the organization.

Here are some basic ground rules for criticism that could make it more productive:

1. As with counseling sessions, it is private and confidential.
2. Don't lose your temper. Let the employee know that he is still considered a valuable and contributing human being.
3. Don't ridicule. We all need to protect our self-image, to save face.
4. Stick to the performance that needs improving; forget about personalities.
5. Get the employee's side of the story. There may be circumstances of which you are unaware.
6. Don't treat a first-time offense as a felony.
7. Let the employee know that he is perfectly normal; we all make mistakes. Let's make the mistake a learning experience.

8. Don't threaten. Management by fear went out in the 1930s. You can't frighten a person into doing a better job.
9. Clearly define the value of correcting the behavior, from a productivity standpoint.
10. Clearly state the performance you expect from here on, and get agreement on it.
11. Let the employee know that your discussion is entirely confidential, so long as you get the results you want.

It is very important that you be both consistent and fair with criticism. If you are, your work group will never resent it. Let there be no exceptions in either your fairness or your consistency. Criticism will not be destructive unless you make it so.

Although this chapter is devoted to the subject of feedback, the activity is not necessarily handled as something separate from other management activities. Feedback is an essential ingredient of coaching, counseling, performance appraisal, and all day-to-day conversations with an employee. It is an ongoing activity through which an employee is kept constantly aware of his performance and any changes needed or expected.

The office manager of an insurance agency had a particularly effective method of providing feedback in a stressfree atmosphere. She would take her employees out to lunch, one at a time, and discuss the job over lunch. This kept the discussion on a completely private basis and employees felt free to discuss every facet of the job. No employee felt singled out when invited to lunch by the manager, wondering what was wrong. It was not a traumatic confrontation and every employee knew she would have a turn at discussing her job.

This manager could see the value of holding such a discussion in a stressfree atmosphere. To an employee, there is always a threat factor inside the office of the boss. Being called into the manager's office for a closed-door meeting always carries an element of embarrassment for an employee. This factor was avoided by holding the discussion over lunch.

Constant feedback is important to every employee in every work situation, whether it is an international sales organization with scores of salesmen or a two- or three-employee work group in a retail store in Arkansas. Employees need to know how they are progressing and performing at all times. Keeping them informed on a continuing basis is a manager's responsibility.

Evaluation of Supervisory Practices (ESP Rating)

1. Do my employees know at all times how their performance compares with expected performance?
2. On a regular basis, do I discuss job requirements with each employee?
3. Are my employees constantly stretching, improving in quantity and quality of output?
4. Do my employees ever ask for more responsibility?
5. Do my employees look forward to a performance appraisal with a positive attitude?
6. Do I avoid discussing personalities during performance appraisals?
7. Do I always criticize privately?
8. Do I deliver criticism in a sensitive manner in order to minimize damage?
9. Do I criticize when it is necessary, rather than avoid it?
10. Am I always fair and consistent with criticism?

9 | Motivating Employees

It has been stated many times that a manager's success depends on his ability to get things done through other people. Why are some supervisors able to get excellent performance from their work groups, while others are barely able to get the job done? Why are some coaches able to produce winning teams consistently, while others remain among the ranks of the losers? Why do some employees continue at a level of mediocrity when we know they are capable of doing better work?

These questions, for the most part, relate to motivation, that moving, driving force or influence that is capable of bringing out the best in all of us. The intent here is to develop an understanding of those factors that cause an employee to excel, and to present some techniques you can apply to move employees toward greater productivity.

There are two big rugs under which the majority of corporate problems have habitually been swept. Whenever things go wrong, the corporate structure tends to attribute the problem either to "poor communications" or to "lack of motivation."

No attempt will be made here to delve into the subject of communications. Rather, we will take a look at motivation from the standpoint of making it more understandable and practical. One

118

certainly doesn't have to be an amateur psychologist to apply practical motivational techniques. Every person in the world has been motivating others since he was born. It didn't take you very long, as a baby, to learn that if you cried loud enough or long enough, you would get a bottle of warm milk shoved into your mouth. You simply motivated your mother. Any time you are influencing another person's behavior, you are motivating that person. Motivation causes behavior.

Motivation is probably one of the most misunderstood, misused, misconstrued management topics we face. Managers scream for it when they already have it. For some reason they tend to equate motivation with excitement, inspiration, enthusiasm. These things relate to motivation, but they are not the same. They can be the manifestation of motivation, but they are not motivation itself.

Managers frequently ask me to come out to the field and hold a meeting to get their people motivated. That is not what the managers are asking for. The employees are already motivated—perhaps in the wrong direction, but motivated they are. It is not a question of whether a person is motivated (one is always motivated); it is a question of whether that motivation is positive or negative. Motivation is like breath. You have it; the question is whether it is good or bad.

Companies frequently look for a "good motivational speaker" for their annual general meeting. In most cases, they are really looking for an inspiring or exciting speaker. Fortunately, the so-called motivational speaker is taking his rightful place in the archives of "has beens"; his efforts did not bring about any significant behavior changes in the job performance of his audience. The audience went away from the meeting excited about the speaker, but nothing new happened on the job.

There is no need to get into a semantic waltz over a definition of "motivation"; it is simply the "thing" that causes certain behavior. Now you can define "thing" any way you want, but, unless some behavior has resulted, there has been no motivation.

When management asks for a great motivational speaker for a

meeting, it should be asked what it wants the audience to do as a result of hearing the speaker. Chances are it won't have an answer. Does it want to excite the group, or to teach it something that will change its behavior? And if it wants to change behavior, what behavior?

The performance model shown as Figure 5 will help you to get a more accurate perspective on the part motivation plays in gaining employee productivity or performance. As can be seen, the left-hand side of the model is made up of two factors—knowledge and the skills necessary to put the knowledge into practice. These are the "can do" factors. They can be taught, and most training programs are built around them.

The right-hand side of the model, too, is made up of two factors—human needs and attitudes. These factors cannot be taught to any degree. They must be provided, and that is a management task. These are the "will do" factors, and are simply referred to as "motivation."

The model is as simple as $2 \times 3 = 6$, which also means that $2 \times$ anything less than $3 =$ less than 6. Also, anything less than $2 \times 3 =$ less than 6. If we are to expect full performance from an employee, both factors of the model must be at peak level. Considering "can do" and "will do" as they relate to employee performance, an overabundance of one will not make up for a deficiency in the other.

For example, an employee with all the knowledge and skill

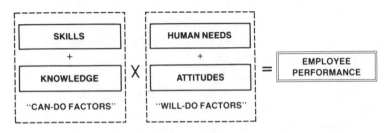

Figure 5. The performance model.

needed, but without the motivation to put them to use, is an "educated slob." On the other hand, an employee who is highly motivated, with a high energy level and lots of enthusiasm, but without any knowledge or skills, is an "excited idiot." Neither of these individuals is going to perform at an acceptable level. Both ability and motivation must be present.

The "can do" factors—skills and knowledge—were discussed in a previous chapter. Training your employees develops both. But you must provide the "will do" factors (motivation). It is your responsibility to "energize" your employees, part of the contractual arrangement you have with your employees.

It has been argued that attitudes should not be included in the model. Many people feel that an attitude is simply the result of something the individual found either motivational or demotivational. It is the frame of mind with which a person approaches a situation, and that frame of mind is determined by the value the person places on that situation. Whether attitudes are a part of motivation or the result, they have an enormous impact on employee behavior.

Let's turn our attention to the right side of the model, and try to develop a practical approach to applying motivational efforts to employees. As a basic foundation for understanding motivation, it is imperative that we establish two premises, basically agreed upon by most leading behaviorists: All behavior is needs oriented, and all behavior is caused.

To put the above in simple terms, everything you do, no matter how rational or irrational it may seem, is to satisfy some basic need you feel at the moment. The need causes the behavior. Therefore, an unsatisfied need is a motivator; it causes behavior. A satisfied need is *not* a motivator; it has no effect on behavior.

Commonly Shared Human Needs

There are five principal needs we all share, and an understanding of these needs is essential in developing a sound method of motivating others. Even though we all share these basic needs, the intensity of each will be different for different people. Also, for every person, the needs are in a constant state of change; they are not static.

To help you understand and conceptualize the five commonly shared human needs, please refer to Figure 6. These needs, which cause behavior, must be satisfied in a logical sequence, from outer needs to inner needs. Needs that exist in the outer area will take precedence over the inner needs, often negating them completely. Let's look at these needs, one at a time.

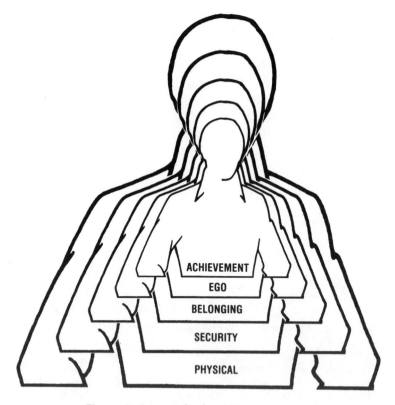

Figure 6. Commonly shared human needs.

Physical needs. These are the basic animal needs shared by everyone. They include the need for food, water, shelter, sex, comfort, rest, and exercise. Until these needs are fairly well satisfied for the individual, the others are of no particular concern. *These* needs will determine behavior. However, once these needs are essentially satisfied, a second set of needs emerges.

Security needs. These include physical, financial, and emotional security—to be protected from bodily harm, to feel unthreatened, to plan for the future, to have job stability, to be free from worry. Many company benefit programs are aimed toward satisfying these needs. Once the individual feels secure, a third set of needs begins to emerge.

The need to belong. This is the human herd instinct. We want to be accepted by others, to be a part of the human race, to be considered a worthwhile individual, to have friends, and to identify with others. When these needs are felt to be nearly satisfied, the fourth set of needs emerges.

Ego needs. These are often called the status needs, or the need to be recognized, but ego needs can be divided into four basic categories:

1. *Ego-building needs.* A sense of self-importance, to be recognized for achievements, to be well thought of by others, to be envied, to be respected.

2. *Ego-defense needs.* To save face, to avoid embarrassment, to protect one's station in life, to be independent, to avoid being dominated by another, to avoid disfavor.

3. *Self-image needs.* To think well of one's self, to have self-confidence, to be attractive to others, to maintain self-respect, and to feel a sense of pride.

4. *The need to dominate.* To be in control of situations, to control others, to have authority, the right to make decisions, and the drive to control the activities of others.

The need to dominate, however, must not be considered only in a negative light. Many people choose a profession or job that allows them to satisfy this need. Consider the schoolteacher, for example. Who is in total control of a classroom? The teacher! The minister is in total control of the congregation. The sales representative is in total control of the sales interview. These are just examples wherein the basic need to dominate *may* have been a strong and unconscious consideration when the profession was chosen.

Once an individual feels his ego needs are essentially satisfied, the final set of needs emerges.

Achievement needs. These are often referred to as the self-fulfillment needs or the self-actualization needs—the drive to be the best, to be the champion, to win, to develop to the fullest potential, to reach the highest peak. Actually there are two types of people identified in this category: There are those who strive to be the best, to have total mastery over their jobs, to be the champion, to excel over others. And there are those who feel a great sense of satisfaction in all the other needs, those who feel they have gotten a lot out of life and want to contribute to others; that is, to put a lot into life. These are often people who quit high-paying jobs to become teachers, ministers, social workers, scout executives, or Peace Corps volunteers. They have a high sense of fulfillment and achievement.

For the most part, the physical needs, security needs, and need to belong are fairly well satisfied in today's society. Most of us are in pretty good physical condition, eat three square meals a day, live comfortably, and enjoy comfortable working conditions. Security needs, too, are covered by pension plans, unions, investments, insurance, tenure, and so on. From a social standpoint, most of us feel well accepted and have our circles of friends, bowling teams, and church groups. There are exceptions, of course, but today's society has taken care of most of the outer needs in the model.

Since the outer needs are basically satisfied, it is obvious that little motivational effort can be applied here. To repeat, a satisfied need is not a motivator. An unsatisfied need is a motivator. Therefore the two inner needs, ego and achievement, become the prime targets for a manager's motivational effort. Motivational effort will be effective *only* when it is directed toward an individual's most dominant unsatisfied needs at the moment. As Mahatma Gandhi once said, "Even God Himself can talk to a hungry man only in terms of bread."

The above illustrates why an employee with severe health problems is unable to reach high levels of achievement. The physical problem (outer need) is the dominant need and attention is turned toward its solution, thereby negating the need to achieve (inner need). First things first.

To illustrate further how needs are satisfied from outer to inner ones, consider a problem that has faced many parents in today's society: drugs. What basic, dominant need prompts a young person to try drugs in the first place? Usually it is the need to belong, to be accepted by his peers, or to have ego protection.

But where is the dominant need rooted when addiction sets in? It is physical. When a person becomes physically addicted to drugs (outer need), what happens to other needs? There are no others of importance to the individual. Security is thrown to the wind as the addict turns to crime to satisfy the physical need. Social aspirations are nonexistent; there is only one person of importance—the addict. Self-respect dies, self-image is destroyed, self-confidence is shattered, and there is no drive to achieve or reach a high level of fulfillment. The basic physical need will shape the behavior pattern totally. The above is a tragic example, but it illustrates the precedence one need will take over another. And a dominant, unsatisfied need is the only target for motivating a person.

Recognizing Motivational Needs

If our motivational efforts must be directed toward an employee's most dominant and unsatisfied needs, how is a manager able to determine what the needs are? A manager has only to be observant and to make a disciplined effort to "read" his employees. As we discussed in a previous chapter, every last one of us has been programmed, just like a computer, by our experiences, rearing, education, and peers.

The manager must study each employee to learn how the employee's card has been punched. He must develop a "motivational profile" of an employee—a basic pattern of the employee's needs. Otherwise, most of his motivational ammunition will miss the target, and little will be achieved.

Every individual constantly (and frequently subconsciously) transmits signals to tell the world his needs. We do so through the things with which we surround ourselves—the cars we drive, the way we live, what we talk about, what we wear, what we join, what we hang on our walls, items of value we place on our desks and bookshelves, and a host of other signals. We are constantly broadcasting our needs to the world. The astute manager must be observant and learn to read the signals.

Bear in mind that needs constantly change; they are not static. What may move a person in one direction today may move that person in the opposite direction tomorrow. The manager must learn to read an employee's usual or typical set of needs in order to develop an effective profile. Never base your profile of an individual on a few isolated signals; watch for a general pattern.

Let's consider some of the typical signals that will help develop a profile, based on each of the commonly shared human needs.

Physical needs. A person whose needs lie predominantly in this area may:

Take excessive sick leave; frequently be late for work
Complain of pain, illness
Feel run down; have a low energy level and no ambition; feel tired most of the time
Be very prone to taking medication, and talk about it frequently
Frequently disregard safe working procedures
Tend to be a "loner"; avoid others
Avoid group activities
Display lack of confidence or a low self-image

Be careless about attire and grooming
Have a generally low work output

How to motivate? Obviously the cause of the problem must be removed, if possible. You may consider sending the employee to the company doctor for a complete physical checkup. Perhaps the employee needs to cut down on smoking or drinking. A jogging or exercise program may help. If the problem is psychosomatic, there may be nothing you can do. Some people suffer beautifully, and enjoy it thoroughly. This is not a physical problem; it is an ego need to gain sympathy or attention.

The person suffering physical needs is usually easy to spot. He usually *looks* sick and run down, shows no ambition, moves slowly, complains, and shows other symptoms. Absentee records show him up quickly and tardiness may become a habit. Regardless of the cause, correction is a must if the employee is to be brought to a productive level.

Remember the sequence in which need satisfaction must occur. As long as the employee's attention is dominated by physical needs, there will be no effort to develop a strong desire to achieve. Productivity will continue to suffer. The employee needs professional help to solve the problem. If he refuses to accept professional help you may have no alternative but to replace him.

Security needs. Emotional insecurity can be caused by many things, but economic insecurity can be just as damaging. Consider the signals of insecurity. The employee:

Is a worrier, doubts his own abilities
In conversation, dwells on poor income, poor standard of living, can't keep up
Lacks confidence, has no self-assuredness
May have problems with creditors
Frequently asks about retirement plan, company insurance programs
May be strong advocate of unionizing
Talks against the company, management, and other employees

Rarely takes risks; may be overly conscious of safety regulations
Rarely volunteers for additional responsibility
May frequently request permission to work overtime
Does not reach decisions readily
May be a procrastinator; puts things off
May be a "loner"; feels uncomfortable around others
Frequently criticizes the way others spend their money
May drive a car several years old
May wear out-of-style clothing
May find it difficult maintaining eye-to-eye contact during
  conversations

What to do? This person needs reassurance that the world is not
coming to an end. A friendly counseling session may help uncover
the cause of the insecurity. Social contacts with peers may help
build confidence. The manager should arrange a few specific job
assignments that have a high chance of success. This person needs
desperately to succeed at something to build some self-confidence,
to begin feeling worthwhile. Perhaps a task-force assignment on a
special project would help.

If the problem is one of economics, perhaps referring the employee to a reliable banker to help him rearrange his budgeting
could get him back on his feet. The manager may be able to arrange for the employee to get some additional overtime work. An
opportunity to enter a company training program to prepare for
advancement could be a strong motivator to the person.

Since reassurance is what the insecure employee needs, frequent contact with the manager is important. A pat on the back,
words of reassurance, a compliment can work wonders. Let the
employee know you still consider him a worthwhile human being.

The need to belong. The person who feels a strong need to be
accepted by others may transmit any of the following signals. He:

May join numerous civic organizations
Is usually very careful about grooming and attire
Is easily led, agrees quickly, tends to "go along with the group"

Tends to interrupt conversations

Likes to organize bowling teams, tennis matches, and other team activities

Is easy to get along with

Readily accepts invitations—to anything

May be a name dropper

Is a conformist—tends to drive a mid-range car, is not a flashy dresser, is somewhat conservative

Exhibits work output that usually ranges from satisfactory to good

Willingly accepts suggestions, criticism, additional responsibility

To motivate this person, a manager must recognize the need to be part of the herd. The manager should provide as many social and group contacts as possible. Task-force assignments work well. Have the employee organize a company softball team, the annual company picnic, or other group events. An invitation to dinner with the manager (spouses included) is a great satisfier. Assign the employee as a "buddy" to a newly hired employee. Invite the employee to sit in on a group or management meeting or planning session. The employee needs to be part of a group. Provide every possible opportunity for it to happen—and on a regular basis.

Ego needs. As we look for a usual profile of this individual, it is important to watch for all four facets of ego needs: ego building, ego defense, self-image, and the need to dominate or control. The signals may vary somewhat.

Before we consider the profile, however, a word about self-image is in order. Each of us has an image we try to project to others; it is the way in which we want others to see us. Furthermore, we will do almost anything to protect or enhance this self-image. Consider, for example, the braggart or the name dropper. What does he hope to gain by such behavior? A feeling of importance, of course; to let others know he has achieved something significant, or travels in important circles. It adds psychological value to the image he is trying to project. Don't condemn the braggart. Rather, try to understand his motives. That person has a strong need to feel valuable, to have you consider him important and worldly.

Why do people adorn their luggage or automobiles with stickers from countries they have visited? It labels them as having been to some exciting place that you may not have visited. Why do people surround themselves with trophies, plaques, and awards? They are visible proof of achievement, and these people have a strong need to let the world know it. They are simply broadcasting signals that say, "Hey, look, folks, I'm an important person; I've achieved something, and I want you to treat me as a somebody."

It's just basic human nature to project to others the image we want them to have of us. The astute manager learns to observe these signals and gain insight into the human needs of his employees. Then he can use accurate motivational techniques that are in tune with the individual's needs. When the manager learns to recognize the signals, he has found that person's motivational triggers. He knows where to apply effort to get results.

The following are frequent signals by those with strong ego needs. The employee:

Displays awards, trophies, plaques
Is a name dropper (people and places)
Usually is a flashy dresser, often nonconforming
May wear expensive jewelry
Drives an overly expensive car
Likes to belong to a country club, and talks about it frequently
Keeps a scrapbook of his achievements
Frequents impressive restaurants
Becomes argumentative if the image is threatened
Does not take criticism well
Seeks greater responsibilities that may provide advancement
Gives advice freely
Prefers being measured against performance standards
Will accept challenging opportunities
May tend to dominate conversations
Is a master of one-upmanship

Takes the lead in group meetings

Gets things done

Tends to be impatient with others who do not meet his standards

Tends to be insensitive toward the feelings of others, including close friends

May tend to antagonize others within a work group and produce disharmony

May seek elective offices, either political or within civic organizations

Again, the person with strong ego needs is not to be condemned, but understood. Many of our greatest achievers are those with strong needs for reinforcement and recognition. They will meet almost any challenge, realizing that they will be recognized for success.

Managing the person with strong ego needs is not difficult. The manager should provide every opportunity for the employee to satisfy these needs. The employee feels a strong need for recognition. The manager should provide challenging assignments that will provide recognition for goals achieved. He should put the employee in charge of task-force or group activities in order to satisfy that urge to control situations.

The manager has an unlimited list of recognition methods available—plaques, trophies, awards, letters of commendation, news releases about the employee's accomplishments, recognition in company or industry publications, a pat on the back, an invitation to dinner (with spouses), praise before peers, ad infinitum. Anything the employee perceives as rewarding will be welcome and effective. Of great value are such things as a special parking space, special privileges, special title, customized business cards, merit increases, stock options, country club membership, and honor societies. The opportunity to gain these plums through achievement serves as a strong motivator. The manager merely provides the opportunity, and then furnishes the deserved recognition.

In a sense it is somewhat difficult to separate those with strong ego needs from those with strong achievement needs. They display many of the same characteristics and signals. But it doesn't matter, because both groups are achievers. One wants the self-satisfaction of achievement; the other wants the recognition that comes from achievement. In either case achievement is the result, and that is what the manager is after.

Achievement needs. There is little difference in the signals broadcast by someone with strong achievement needs and someone with strong ego needs. Here are some possibilities for those with strong achievement needs:

Very fashionable dresser, but somewhat conservative
Less outspoken than one with ego needs
Less dependent upon others; can work alone
Introverted in some cases
Patient with others
Very secure, the picture of self-confidence
Feels independent
Requires minimum supervision
Readily accepts delegation
Usually analytical in thinking

What this person needs is a constant flow of challenging assignments and opportunities. Free rein in the job is very important, with minimum close supervision. It is important for this employee to feel a great sense of independence in performing the job. Over-managing demotivates this person.

It would be impossible to include in this book all the many signals people broadcast to tell the world their needs. Nor would it be possible to include the multitude of things a manager can do to help his employees satisfy their needs. The manager must *observe* and *respond* if he is to get the behavior desired.

Repeating a word of caution. It is extremely important for a manager to look for a pattern of signals when trying to determine an employee's motivational profile. Never attempt to identify the profile from single or isolated signals. Watch for a general pattern. If a manager gets to know his employees well, he can develop a profile that will approximate accuracy. Things are not always as predictable as they may look, however. Behavior is very complicated and complex, and the manager must understand its complexity before he can keep it channeled in acceptable and productive patterns.

The Behavioral Cycle

When a need exists, behavior will follow—but it will not always be predictable. Why? Because an individual has many behavioral options available to help satisfy needs. One cannot always predict the optional behavior the person will select. Let's look at a simple example of the behavioral options:

Let's say, for example, the need (stimulus) is hunger. To satisfy this need a person has to eat. But there are many ways of getting something to eat, some socially acceptable, some not. There are several options open: Buy food, steal food, grow food (if a person is not too hungry, and can wait), beg for food, trade for food, or work for food. Although this is a simplified example, it illustrates the variety of options open.

The point is, we are constantly bombarded with options when we have needs to satisfy. It is the manager's job to channel his employees' behavior into acceptable, profitable, and proper channels. That requires an understanding of the behavioral cycle shown as Figure 7: how it works, the pitfalls, and the options involved. It is a complex mechanism.

To understand the cycle and the part the manager plays in channeling behavior, let's examine the complete model of the cycle, and study the process through which an individual goes in selecting behavior. The behavioral cycle also extends our understanding of motivation as it relates to a manager's job; that is, how he uses it to guide behavior into acceptable channels. It will explain why we tend to select certain patterns of behavior, and why there are so many behavioral options available. Let's follow the cycle, step by step:

Stimulus. A need has been created. The stimulus may have

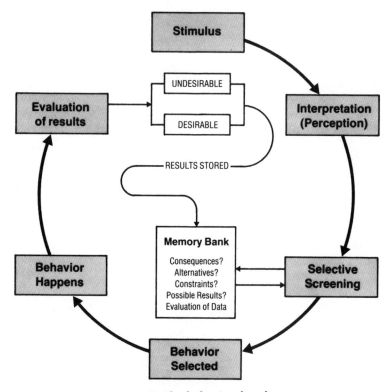

Figure 7. The behavioral cycle.

come from within the individual or it may have been provided by someone or something else. Perhaps, during a counseling session, the manager encouraged an employee to improve in the job, to reach for greater achievement. Perhaps the smell of a sirloin steak turned on a need. We are constantly bombarded by stimuli, both from within and from without, and this is where behavior starts. A need has been created and some form of behavior will occur, because all behavior is need oriented and all behavior is caused.

Interpretation. This may be called perception; that is, how the individual perceives the meaning of the stimulus. Perhaps the stimulus was a phone call from the boss, saying, "Tom, I want you in my office at 2 o'clock this afternoon." The first thing that comes to Tom's mind (interpretation) is, "I wonder what he wants." Identification or interpretation of the stimulus is the first step toward selecting an appropriate behavior.

Selective screening. The selective screening process is the one in which the identified stimulus is run through the "memory bank" in order to match it with an appropriate behavior. This process may take place in a fraction of a second, or it may take hours or days of pondering. No modern data processing system can compare with the human mind. Stored in this memory bank is everything we have learned, heard, smelled, tasted, thought, read, touched, seen, and experienced. It's all there, although at times some of it is difficult to retrieve. The memory bank is the total of all our experiences—our total programming.

The stimulus interpretation is fed into the memory bank, and the selection process begins. As various behavioral options are considered, many factors are weighed:

Consequences. What happens if I do? What happens if I don't? What will the outcome be? Will it be good? Bad? Is it going to be worth it? What's in it for me?

Alternatives. Is there something better for me to do? Is there something I'd rather do? Would something else produce a more desirable outcome? Is this what he really wants? Is this what I really want?

Constraints. These are our built-in policemen. They protect us from improper behavior (at times). Many constraints are imposed on us, both from within and from without. There are social, legal, ethical, economic, religious, policy, moral, and a host of self-imposed constraints. These are our inhibitors, and they have a great bearing on our behavior selection patterns.

Possible results. As the various constraints are considered, the resulting outcome is studied. Then a trip may be made back to the alternatives and back again to the constraints, with all factors weighed and considered.

Evaluation. Finally, all factors of the memory bank are analyzed and compared with the possible outcome. Then—*behavior is selected*—and—*action begins.* But the cycle is not yet complete.

Evaluation of results. If the results of the behavior turn out to be favorable (rewarding), the information is immediately fed into the memory bank to provide guidance for future selection of behavior. If the behavior turns out to be undesirable (punishing or nonrewarding), that information is also stored in the memory bank for future reference, to serve as an inhibitor or self-imposed constraint to keep us from repeating the mistake. But when unfavorable results are fed into the memory bank, the alternatives are again considered as possible corrective measures. We may find an alternative that will produce more desirable results.

The Manager's Role

The true value in management lies in providing as many opportunities as possible for desirable behavior, and then reinforcing that behavior. The reinforcement makes the person aware that the outcome was favorable. Each of these desirable experiences will be fed into the memory bank for future use. Obviously, the more there are, the more the employee can call on in future selective screening. It's all part of acquired wisdom.

The manager must also provide immediate consequences for undesirable behavior, for these, too, will be fed into the memory bank—and inhibit repetition of the undesirable behavior.

As we study the principles of positive reinforcement in the next chapter, we will see the tremendous impact a manager has in developing the proper information in an employee's memory bank.

Summary

When we consider the plasticity of a person's motivational profile and see that it is in a constant state of change because needs are variable, it becomes obvious that leadership must be variable, too. Motivational efforts applied must be in tune with the needs of the individual that are predominant at the moment.

Actually, the only leadership style that is worth its salt is a flexible style, one that is in tune with the needs of the individual. And that style may run the full spectrum—from autocratic to free rein—within a day. We all tend to respond favorably (both mentally and physically) to people and situations we perceive as helping us satisfy our needs. Happiness is the sensation we feel when our needs have been satisfied. Unhappiness is felt when that satisfaction has been denied or an undesirable need has been created.

You do not have true motivation until the employee does a better job because he wants to do a better job. This situation can be created by a manager who recognizes that an employee's performance depends on the *manager's* input to the employee's memory bank—the provision of recognition for reinforcement of positive behavior and inhibitors or constraints for negative behavior. All the reinforcements and constraints will be available to the employee for reference as he considers behavioral options. A good manager will see that plenty of the right material is on file in the bank. That's the manager's responsibility in developing people.

Evaluation of Supervisory Practices (ESP Rating)

1. Do I create a climate in which achievement is possible and recognize that achievement in a positive manner?
2. Do I constantly look for an employee's unsatisfied needs in order to determine his motivational "triggers"?
3. Do I attempt to "read" my employees regularly in order to identify their usual motivational profile?
4. Do I recognize the signals of physical needs?
5. Do I recognize the signals of security needs?
6. Do I recognize the signals of one who needs to belong?
7. Do I recognize the signals of ego needs?
8. Do I recognize the signals of achievement needs?

9. Do I have a motivational plan for each of the five commonly shared needs?
10. Do I constantly reinforce desirable behavior?
11. Do I provide negative consequences immediately for undesirable behavior?
12. Do I maintain a flexible style of management in tune with the current needs of each employee?

10 | Positive Reinforcement

Reinforcement is the manager's reactions to an employee's actions. Think about this; it is an extremely important but often overlooked or neglected management responsibility. Behavior must be reinforced if it is to be continued or repeated. Even desirable behavior that receives no reinforcement tends not to be repeated.

The reinforcement (feedback) the employee receives from the manager will help determine whether the behavior will be repeated. If the employee finds the reinforcement favorable or rewarding (positive consequence) the behavior will tend to strengthen and be repeated. If the employee finds the reinforcement unfavorable, unrewarding, or punishing (negative consequence), the behavior will tend not to be repeated. To give no positive reinforcement produces the same result as negative reinforcement. It develops a "who cares?" attitude.

Right along with the need for a favorable self-image is our need for positive reinforcement from others. The normal person likes to be liked by others. Praise, commendation, and appreciation from others is important to him. Whether the person is an executive, janitor, truck driver, or production employee, he wants to know how he is doing.

Some people say "I don't care what other people think of me," but they don't really mean it. What other people think does matter. Even the most mature person is eager to get positive feedback so that he knows where he stands and what adjustments he should make to improve his performance. Favorable attention and favorable reinforcement from others and from himself may be the mainstays of his personal development. When a person fails to get positive reinforcement, he tends to:

Feel rejected, feel unappreciated
Feel he doesn't know how well he is doing
Feel left out and become a loner
Feel inadequate, frustrated, discouraged
Be uncooperative and not participate
Have no purpose for being and become a rebel
Lose pride, stagnate, and stop trying
Seem unable to plan ahead
Feel that no one respects him as a person
Develop an unfavorable self-image

Again, this kind of situation has a terrific impact on how well he does his job and his attitude toward his work. Lack of positive reinforcement has a direct correlation to the quality of his work. Nothing hurts more than being ignored. Not to be seen, recognized, heard, or noticed is like not being there at all. Does your employee know you know he is there?

It doesn't take a professional psychologist to understand that these are the basic "guts" of human relations, the very foundation of motivation. They develop within the employee a sense of pride in what he is doing, spur him to greater achievement, and give him a feeling that he's really important to the organization. They help him put his work in a proper perspective. Your positive reinforcement provides data for the employee's memory bank, data that will affect his future behavior.

You feed the reinforcement into the employee's memory bank by seeing to it that something happens (called consequences) when the employee's behavior deviates from satisfactory performance.

But it is essential that the consequences used are *appropriate*. Even employees whose behavior is right up to standard need positive reinforcement.

It is important not to think of deviation as negative. Deviation refers to any behavior (negative or positive) that falls outside the area of expected performance. We strive toward positive deviations; that's our objective in improving performance. We want high achievers—the positive deviants. They accomplish and achieve *more* than is expected.

Selecting Appropriate Consequences

Regardless of your school of thought on establishing consequences for the improvement, change, or correction of behavioral patterns in people, it may be difficult for you to agree with everything presented in this chapter. The disagreements, however, will principally be a matter of semantics, although there may be some disagreement regarding hypotheses presented and conclusions drawn. Our objective is to determine consequences that lead employees toward improved productivity.

I dislike the terms "reward" and "punishment," because they imply that there are only two directions we can go in changing behavior. Instead, I am going to restrict the key terms to "negative consequences" and "positive consequences." It is too easy to get into a semantic dither over "reward" and "punishment" and which is which. For example:

Boss: "If you don't do it my way, I'll beat the hell out of you!" (punishment)
Boss: "If you do it my way, I promise *not* to beat the hell out of you!" (Reward)

See what I mean? I'll leave it up to you to separate the rewards from the punishments. I'll stick to negative and/or positive consequences.

Simply stated, a positive consequence is an outcome the employee perceives as being favorable or desirable. A negative consequence is perceived as being unfavorable, undesirable, or of no particular value to the individual.

The concept of positive versus negative consequences invalidates the "no news is good news" philosophy. If desirable behavior receives no reinforcement, the behavior tends *not* to be repeated. Why? Because there was no payoff for the behavior; it produced nothing rewarding. Therefore, the behavior had no value to the individual, personal satisfaction notwithstanding.

If a manager wishes to see desirable behavior repeated he must reinforce it continually. Not to do so would discourage repetition. The immediacy of the reinforcement, too, is important. Reinforcement that is too late in coming loses much of its value. This is another reason it is important for a manager to maintain regular and frequent contact with his employees. When desirable behavior occurs the manager is there to provide timely reinforcement. The same is true for both positive and negative consequences; the more immediate it is, the more valuable it is in establishing a pattern for subsequent behavior.

It may be well to lay a little groundwork to get started in the right direction, especially for a manager who has not yet delved into the field of performance discrepancies. You may prefer to call them deficiencies, differences, or deviations rather than discrepancies. Have it your way.

When an employee is not performing the way we want, it is because of either a discrepancy in knowledge—he simply doesn't know how to do the job—or a discrepancy in execution—he knows how, but doesn't do it the way he should, or as well, or as completely, or as fast. At any rate, the employee isn't doing it to suit the boss.

If the discrepancy is a question of insufficient knowledge, training is needed. Most training programs are designed to close the knowledge and skills gap.

If, however, the problem is one of execution, some action must be taken to get behavior back on a known track. It is generally agreed that a discrepancy in execution is caused by one or more of three things:

1. *Lack of feedback* to the employee regarding the performance. The employee may not be aware of the deviation, place little importance on it, or not really know what is expected.

2. *Task interference* on the job. There are aspects of the job or working environment that make it difficult or impossible for the employee to perform satisfactorily and are not the employee's fault. These obstacles need to be removed.

3. *Inappropriate consequences* when performance deviates from the expected (nothing happens, too much happens, or the wrong thing happens).

It is toward the selection of appropriate consequences that this chapter will address itself.

The behavioral spectrum, shown as Figure 8, will help you conceptualize the approaches to behavioral changes. Let's begin with this model, which illustrates both negative and positive behavioral deviation.

You'll notice that the area of expected performance (usually established through performance standards) allows for some minor negative deviations from the norm. We expect employees to make minor mistakes; we accept them; we allow employees to function a little below satisfactory levels at times for various reasons. That does not mean we let it happen without consequences.

The sole purpose of providing consequences (in any case) is to move the employee's behavior toward the upper end of the spectrum. Naturally, the area of expected performance is not the same for all employees. All motivational efforts are aimed toward the same goal, however. Action taken within the lower side of the spectrum is generally considered as corrective or disciplinary in nature. For simplicity, you may wish to consider consequences in the upper half of the spectrum as generally positive or motivational (rewards, if you prefer); and consequences in the lower half as generally negative or corrective (punishment, if you prefer).

The appropriate selection of positive consequences should be in

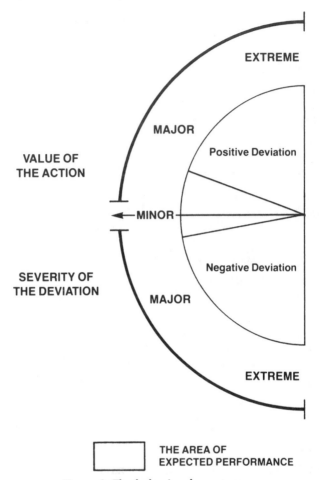

Figure 8. The behavioral spectrum.

proportion to the value of the employee's action. You wouldn't give an employee the "Man of the Year" award simply because he got to work on time each morning. That's overdoing it. Negative consequences must also be in proportion to the severity of the deviation. Unfortunately, consequences (especially the negative ones) are frequently way out of proportion. How often has an employee been fired for minor infractions simply because the boss was in a bad mood at the time? Too often.

Bear in mind that negative consequences are not limited to the lower half of the spectrum; nor are positive consequences limited to the upper half. We may apply positive consequences to change an employee's deviation severity from major to minor. At times, we may apply negative consequences to disturb employee complacency and move him from one valuable performance to one of greater value.

Almost any professional manager will agree that consequences must always be provided throughout the behavior spectrum, including the area of expected performance. This truism is often violated. Many managers step in to provide consequences (negative) only when things go wrong.

As a matter of fact, the philosophy of "management by exception" can foster this kind of action at times. Under the philosophy of "management by exception" the manager pretty well stays out of the picture until employee performance deviates on the negative side. He then steps in for corrective action. Although the philosophy does place some emphasis on reinforcement, the major stress seems to be "When anything goes wrong—step in."

Some managers tend to deal in extremes, too, overdoing the consequences. This is especially tragic on the negative side of the scale. For example, a manager who believes that no one likes to work and everyone must be driven to get a job done tends to deal in negative extremes because of his basic attitudes. But if you treat a man like a bum, he'll behave like a bum. This manager tends to ignore positive consequences for the same reason. The manager who has an erroneous concept of himself and of others may well fit into this category, too.

A manager who believes that people like to work and that working is as natural as breathing tends to go in the opposite direction. Obviously, both managers need a balance of consequences. On the behavior spectrum, there is no neutral zone. Consequences should always be provided. They provide an important feedback to the employee regarding his performance, whether negative or positive.

Factors Affecting Appropriateness

In determining whether consequences (negative or positive) are appropriate, many factors must be considered. You may be familiar with the standard army answer to any tactical question, "It depends on the terrain and the situation." The same is true here. Appropriateness depends mainly on the employee, the manager, and the situation. But it doesn't stop here. A lengthy list of other factors must be considered:

The severity of the negative deviation. Overreacting here can easily cause unpredictable behaviors. When faced with a threatening situation, an employee has several behavioral options available to protect himself. You might even get a fist in the mouth. If he feels the consequence was not in proportion to the offense, the employee might do anything. Some of his options include physical abuse, verbal abuse, lying, stealing (to strike back), organizing a union for protection, rationalization, quitting the job, bad publicity, withdrawal, alcohol, or suicide. Don't laugh, it has happened. Any way you look at it, a minor infraction deserves a minor consequence. Remember: "Let the punishment fit the crime."

The value of the positive deviation. Most motivational programs and material seem to deal in the area of positive consequences. Again, the reward should be commensurate with the performance. Don't overdo it. One of the best examples of overdoing it is with idle flattery. Such flattery soon becomes meaningless to the employee.

Frequency of deviation. Negative consequences should become more severe for the habitual offender. At the same time, positive consequences should become greater for the habitual achiever. They are the motivator.

Employee's awareness of the deviation. Don't provide the consequence until the employee is aware that performance was something less (or more) than expected. This is especially true for the employee who has never been provided an accurate job description or a set of meaningful performance standards. In such cases the quality control aspects of the job have been delegated to the employee. It is questionable whether a manager has any moral right to criticize such an employee.

Job level of the employee. Certainly rank has its privileges. As an employee climbs the corporate ranks, latitude should be given for mistakes (or negative deviations). We expect growing employees to go out on a limb, and this must be considered in determining consequences for deviation.

We've often heard it said, "If he doesn't make some mistakes, he isn't doing his job." I just wonder whether we really believe that. Generally, the higher the employee is in the corporate hierarchy, the more readily he will react to *minor* negative consequences. The employee is usually more sensitive to subtle discipline, and is usually a pretty high achiever or he wouldn't be coming up the corporate ladder.

Effect on the rest of the organization. Selecting inappropriate consequences (negative or positive) could easily create problems among other employees. They may consider the consequence unfair to the employee involved or to themselves. Consider the effect on the group when it feels a fellow employee was discharged or disciplined unfairly. It creates morale problems and can easily reduce the productivity of the entire group.

On the other hand, overreacting on the positive side of the scale can create resentment and intergroup conflicts. For example, how does the production line employee react when he sees a salesman win a three-day trip to Acapulco? In the first place, he feels the salesman is overpaid and underworked, and that the opposite is true for him. He feels that quality manufacturing was what made the product sell in the first place.

This example does not represent overreacting on the positive side of the scale except to the production line employee. The salesman may feel he should have been given two weeks in Acapulco rather than three days. Everything is relative to one's own position in life.

Attitude of the employee. How does the employee feel about the appropriateness of the consequence? Did he deserve more (or less)? Was it fair? Perhaps negative deviation had more far-reaching effects on the company than even the employee realized. Was he aware of the effects? Was he working within narrower parameters? Maybe it wasn't as big a deal to the employee as it was to upper management, which had the advantage of the "big picture." Is the consequence appropriate in the eyes of management or in the eyes of the employee? The answer should be both.

Consistency of consequences used in the organization. It doesn't take a professional psychologist to understand that consistency is the rule in disciplining or rewarding a child. "Once in a while" doesn't get the job done. There must be a consistent correlation between performance and consequences (either negative or positive). An employee may tolerate stern discipline once in a while very well, knowing he will get by with his enjoyable deviation the next ten times. A manager who practices inconsistency can neither train nor expect consistently favorable behavior. Consistency means the same treatment for all employees under the same circumstances. You cannot give one employee the privilege of deviating and not give the same privilege to his peers, all other things being equal.

The employee's perception of the cause. Perhaps there were extenuating circumstances. The employee may feel the deviation was completely (or partially) justified. He should certainly be given an opportunity to voice an opinion. Otherwise, the consequence is likely to seem completely inappropriate to him. If so, the reacting behavior could be inappropriate to the manager's purpose.

On the positive deviation side, the employee may feel his actions were worth far more than the manager does. He may feel he went completely above and beyond the call of duty and incurred certain self-inflicted inconveniences in order to get the job done. If the manager sees the action as less valuable, the consequence will probably be inappropriate. This could easily serve to discourage the employee from "going all out" the next time. Again, inappropriate consequences have a negative effect on behavior.

The manager's mood at the time. Frequently, negative consequences are inappropriate and are caused by a manager losing his temper and overreacting. A series of little incidents may pile up, causing the manager to vent his anger all at once. The manager may then apply an extreme consequence for an insignificant deviation.

On the positive side, the manager may overreward as a result of a series of actions (not necessarily a bad policy) when the employee is focusing on a single action. If the reward is for multiple actions, that should be explained to the employee, so he understands the appropriateness.

A manager may select inappropriate consequences (or fail even to provide any) simply because he is in a particularly good mood at the time. In the eyes of the employees, lack of action may be taken as inconsistency or as favoritism toward a particular employee.

The manager's attitude toward the employee. We seem to enjoy kicking someone we don't like and overrewarding our favorites. It's human nature. But a manager must maintain fairness and consistency at all times. A manager may overlook a good employee's infractions at times because he is a good producer. Who doesn't? But the manager may tend, also, to overlook the good performance of an employee who has a normal reputation for generally poor performance.

Inappropriate consequences may also be selected because of bigotry, prejudice, or personality. Young, liberal employees often clash with older, ultraconservative managers. Minority employees are frequently victims of inappropriate treatment (negative and positive) for the same reason—manager attitude.

Peer pressure. Is the deviation caused by pressure from the employee's peer group? Does the group feel that particular employee is bucking for a promotion that might make it look bad? Is the employee striking back at the peer group for some reason?

The manager's preference for certain consequences for himself. The manager naturally feels that "what's good for the goose is good for the gander." The consequences the manager feels affect his performance most may become favorites when he is dealing with other people. He may assume that what motivates him will motivate others, an attitude that may be completely inappropriate.

The motivational factors of the employee must be considered in selecting appropriate negative or positive consequences.

An individual's needs, from a motivational standpoint, frequently dictate the appropriate style of consequences. Let's concentrate on the negative deviation side of the spectrum. Motivational needs will dictate the type of consequence, not the severity. Severity should be commensurate with the degree of deviation.

Before we proceed further with the discussion of appropriateness of consequences, a couple of definitions are in order:

Psychological consequence: Threatened negative consequence (punishment) or promised positive consequence (reward).

Tangible consequence: Threatened or promised consequence actually carried out or administered.

High achiever: One whose behavior generally lies above the area of expected performance in the performance deviation model shown in Figure 9.

Low achiever: One whose behavior generally lies in the lower 50 percent of the performance deviation model.

As we correlate this model with the behavior spectrum and the model of commonly shared human needs discussed in Chapter 9, some interesting hypotheses begin to develop:

Hypothesis 1. High achievers consider negative consequences opportunities to move up in the behavior spectrum. Psychological consequences, both negative and positive, are viewed as a challenge.

Hypothesis 2. Low achievers consider negative consequences a threat to physical welfare and security. The main exception is the financially affluent slob who doesn't like to work.

Hypothesis 3. Managers generally reserve positive consequences for high achievers and negative ones for low achievers.

The main reason high achievers respond better to consequences in the area of inner needs is because that is where their motives lie. To an employee who is hungry for recognition, the promise of

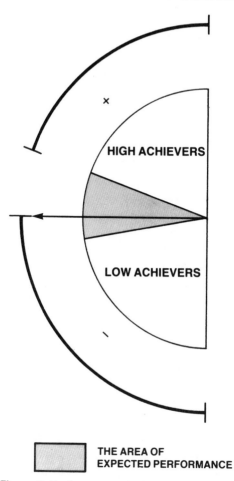

Figure 9. Performance deviation model.

recognition or threat of losing recognition is a very real factor in changing behavior.

Therefore, an understanding of an employee's motivational needs is the key to selecting appropriate consequences. This key is often overlooked in negative deviations. We tend to love high achievers and hate low achievers. That alone tends to jaundice our selection of appropriate consequences (hypothesis 3).

Hypothesis 4. The motivational needs of low achievers are generally found in the physical, security, and need-to-belong categories (outer needs).

To illustrate the argument for hypothesis 4: Low achievers are generally that way because of lack of self-confidence, lack of education, lack of ambition, defeatist attitudes, antisocial attitudes, and poor self-image (often created by the above). As a result they seldom move to higher level jobs where it becomes important to reach toward recognition, status, or achievement. They often resign themselves to their lot in life, and they don't want to lose it. They are predestined failures, and treat themselves that way.

The only meaningful negative consequence to these people is the threat of losing what little they have (usually tangible). Conversely, the most effective positive consequence is the promise of more of what they have.

Hypothesis 5. A low achiever can be brought to a high level of achievement, not in one grand jump, but through a carefully planned succession of negative and positive consequences, one level of needs at a time.

Hypothesis 6. The motivational needs of high achievers are generally found in the areas of ego and achievement.

Hypothesis 7. Please burn this one into your mind! If, through your leadership style, you are generating feelings of insecurity among your employees, those people are psychologically incapable of developing a strong drive to achieve. (Now, please reread what was just said, and think about it.) Based on the sequential order in which needs cause behavior, all the employee's effort will be directed toward the security needs, negating any effort toward achievement. Here is where we see the counterproductive effect of autocratic managers. The style works against the objective.

We regularly see examples of inappropriate negative and positive consequences. And the managers applying them rarely recognize the counterproductive effects they have on the work group. Before selecting any consequence, a manager should ask several questions:

How severe is the negative deviation, or how valuable is the positive deviation?

How frequently does it occur?

Does the employee realize he has deviated?

Will it affect the rest of the organization in a favorable way?

Why did the deviation take place?

Is there any task interference causing it?

What is the employee's side of the story?

Am I in the right mood to select an appropriate consequence?

How do I feel toward the employee in general?

Is the consequence really appropriate, or is it only my favorite one?

What are the employee's motivational needs right now?

Note: It is important to remember, when handling discipline with union employees, to follow established labor procedures. Read your labor agreement.

Examples of Effective Consequences

In the following examples you will find many that could, and should, be listed under several groups of needs. There is a great amount of overlap, so the items are not cast in concrete. You will also find fewer negatives in the first set of needs, simply because high achievers command fewer consequences that are negative. Conversely, subsequent needs will contain a different balance because the low achievers have a different balance of needs from a motivational standpoint.

The list of possible consequences is endless, but these may serve to trigger your thinking and give you a starting point. Naturally, all employees must have the pat on the back, reassurance, opportunity for advancement, adequate (fair) earnings, and so on. By no means is the following list all-inclusive, but it will give you some ideas regarding both positive and negative consequences that can be used to modify behavior:

FOR EMPLOYEES WITH ACHIEVEMENT NEEDS

Positive Consequences

Greater responsibilities (vertical loading of the job)

Special assignments

Leading task forces

Additional training for job advancement

Educational assistance programs

Sabbatical leave for education

Teaching assignments

First-place awards

Certificates of completion or achievement

Negative Consequences

Simply advise of your displeasure

A frown of disapproval

Routine questions regarding performance, such as "Don't you feel you can do better?"

Subtle indicators of disappointment

Simply question the deviations.

Point out that he is setting a poor example for others

Remove from special assignments

Suspend training for advancement

FOR EMPLOYEES WITH EGO NEEDS

Positive Consequences

All those previously listed

Plaques, trophies, and awards

Commendation letters

Special titles

Ask for advice

Allow to serve as assistant supervisor

Special projects

Speaking assignments

Public relations work

Participation in committees

Allow to serve on management council

Stock options

Merit increases

Country club membership

Incentive trips or awards

Honor societies

Publicity in media

Praise before peers and management

Negative Consequences

All those previously listed

"Bringing up the rear" award

Verbal reprimand

Reduce awards offered

Publish results of accomplishments (with all others, of course)

Bypass for management training class

Remove special privileges

Remove special parking space

Assign "coffeepot" detail

Have him work Saturday on his own time

Silent treatment for a short time (the ego-centered individual can't stand to be ignored)

Positive Consequences
Published results of accom-
plishments
Involve spouse in awards
Management development op-
portunities
Special parking space
Company blazer

FOR EMPLOYEES WITH A NEED TO BELONG

Positive Consequences	*Negative Consequences*
Membership in special clubs	All those previously listed
Captain of bowling team	Remove from organized activities
Invitation to dinner, including spouse	Invite to dinner, without spouse, for discussion of performance
Invitation to management party or meeting	Pass up with invitation to management party
Transfer to larger group	Transfer to smaller group
Assignment as "buddy" to a new employee	Disqualify for participation in some incentives
Ask to organize softball or other team	Remove from special assignments
Supervisory assignments	
Task-force assignments	
Committee assignments	

FOR EMPLOYEES WITH SECURITY NEEDS

Positive Consequences	*Negative Consequences*
Salary increases	All those previously listed
Stock options	Salary freeze or decrease
Participation in insurance program	Eliminate stock options
Bonus program	Reduce or eliminate bonus
Tenure program	Demotion
Frequent reassurance	Transfer to lesser job
Keep employee informed on all matters possible	Frown
Promotions	Reprimand (varying degrees)
	Suspension

Positive Consequences	Negative Consequences
Frequent counseling regarding accomplishments	Ignore (silent treatment)
	Probation
Smile	Coaching session (severe)
Pat on the back	Work on Saturday on his own time
Commendation before peers	
Discussion of employee's future	Threat of termination (as last resort only)
Congratulatory letters	

FOR EMPLOYEES WITH PHYSICAL NEEDS

Positive Consequences	Negative Consequences
Salary increases	Suspension
Stock options	Salary decrease
Bonus program	Demotion
Cash incentives	Removal of bonus program
Promotion opportunities	Transfer
Offer training for advancement	Verbal disciplining
Improved working conditions	Strong counseling session
Opportunities for extra overtime pay	Reprimand (varying degrees)
	Work overtime, with no overtime pay
Reassurance	
Regular physical checkups	Probation
Participation in recreational activities	Termination (as last resort only)
Bonus to quit smoking	

A *word of caution:* The application of many consequences, both negative and positive, for unionized employees will be governed by contract; for example, you may not be able to make him work overtime without extra pay. Always consult your labor agreement concerning union groups.

Negative Consequences

It is argued by many that the application of *any* type of negative consequence is poor management practice. That may sound philosophical, but let's face reality. There are times when negative consequences are necessary. Positive consequences are always better—if they work. When they fail to bring about the desired behavior, there is no alternative but to go to the negatives. But always be certain that consequences are appropriate for the occasion, whether they be positive or negative.

Good Judgment

Good judgment will usually help a manager avoid problems in establishing consequences. When we speak of positive consequences, we are usually speaking of motivational techniques. In the majority of cases, the subtle pat on the back, a smile, words of encouragement, and congratulations before the employee's peers will work wonders. On the negative consequence side, a simple frown, a question about quality of performance, or subtle dissatisfaction will usually suffice. Naturally, in extreme or habitual cases sterner measures must be taken.

Most managers find the positive consequences pretty easy to pass around (although there are too many exceptions to this), but the negatives are easy to ignore. It's typical to feel, "If I just ignore this little problem, maybe it will go away." But it doesn't go away; little things pile up, and finally (when the manager is in a bad mood) all hell breaks loose. The manager loses his temper, overreacts, goes to an extreme in selecting disciplinary measures, and damages both the employee and his performance. The inappropriateness often builds peer group resentment, and group productivity suffers.

A good employee is like a piece of equipment. You make each repair as the malfunction occurs, rather than wait until it's ready for the scrap heap to start rebuilding or replacing it. Negative consequences provide the repairs. Positive consequences provide the fuel and lubricant to keep it running smoothly. But, just as with the equipment, you have to use the right fuel, the right lubricant, and the right repairs. You would never try to repair a wristwatch with a sledgehammer. But we see managers using that kind of technique on their employees. It's inappropriate. Select the right

158	Shirt-Sleeves Management

tool for the right job at the right time, and your machinery and people will run better, smoother, and more productively.

Consequences of Inappropriate Consequences

In order to illustrate the undesirable outcomes of inappropriate consequences, it is essential that we refer back to the model of the behavioral cycle in Chapter 9 (Figure 7), as it relates to the outcome or results of the employee's actions being stored for future use as a reinforcement for repetition or constraint against repetition. The appropriateness of consequences may dictate *how* the employee will store and use that information in the future.

In order to establish the proper constraints against inappropriate behavior and the proper reinforcements for appropriate behavior, meaningful and proper consequences must be provided. If the consequences are inappropriate, the storing will also be inappropriate. As with a computer, "garbage in, garbage out."

Appropriate positive consequences are viewed by the employee as fair. They satisfy his needs, provide a learning experience, and promote repetition of the behavior that earned the consequence. If inappropriate, they breed resentment and frustration, and serve as a constraint against initiative. If overdone, they can establish costly precedents and will be viewed as insincere.

Appropriate negative consequences are also viewed as fair and as a learning experience, and serve as a constraint against repetition. If inappropriate, they serve as a constraint against initiative, and cause resentment and frustration (if overdone). If too little negative consequence is provided, it is easily ignored and fails to establish the necessary constraint against repetition.

Summary

Providing appropriate consequences is the direct responsibility of the manager in all cases of behavioral deviation, whether negative or positive. Selecting the most appropriate consequence for the situation at hand requires several considerations. The material contained in this chapter should give you some helpful guidance in the selection of consequences that will improve the performance of your subordinates, the people who look to you for guidance, encouragement, and correction. Every employee sincerely wants to do a good job. It is your responsibility to provide the guidance needed. Consequences, if appropriate, form a very important part of that guidance.

Finally, give that employee the positive reinforcement he needs to gain momentum. Use that pat on the back, that kind word, that arm on the shoulder, that little word of encouragement. We all seek approval from others, especially from the boss. Achievement that goes unrecognized serves as a demotivator and inhibits a drive to improve. Don't let sheer oversight on your part become a demotivator. When was the last time you told one of your employees that you were proud of him? Do it more often.

Evaluation of Supervisory Practices (ESP Rating)

1. Do I provide a consequence regularly when behavior deviates from expected norms?
2. Do I perceive "deviation" in both a positive and negative way?
3. Do I provide minor consequences, consistently, for minor infractions?
4. Do I avoid overrewarding for positive deviations?
5. Do I consider as many pertinent factors as possible before selecting consequences?
6. Do I consider the employee's side of the story before selecting negative consequences?
7. Am I fair and consistent with all employees?
8. Do I avoid any management style that might generate feelings of insecurity among my employees?
9. Do I use more positive than negative consequences?
10. Do I frequently tell my employees, "I'm proud of you"— and mean it?

11 | Encouragement and Expectation

This seems, perhaps, to be an extension of the previous chapter on positive reinforcement. However, the subject is of sufficient significance to stand alone. Your personal, sincere, and regular encouragement is a constant source of fuel to your employees. But there is a significant factor that may dictate how well you encourage your employees—your expectations.

By expectations, I don't mean how much work you expect or want the employee to do. Expectation is what you honestly, genuinely, and sincerely believe the employee is capable of achieving. It is your faith in the employee, not your awareness of the workload. Your expectations have a direct and positive bearing both in establishing objectives and in motivating employees to higher productivity. You must have faith in your employees; you must believe in them. Your faith and belief must be transmitted loudly and clearly to every one of them.

Most employees are capable of far more than they do. Their productivity and growth, however, may be inhibited by several factors. They may be working under a manager who is incapable of assessing their potential, their talents, and their desire to grow objectively. The manager may see them as incapable and treat them as incapables. He may be unwilling to delegate because of

160

his own insecurity, feeling that he is protecting his job by inhibiting the growth of subordinates. But the development of subordinates is an important management responsibility. Never jeopardize your own chance of advancement by having a weak subordinate behind you.

Your expectation of an employee will determine the way you manage that employee. If you feel he is unambitious, unimaginative, and low in skills and knowledge (whether true or not), you will tend to overmanage, spend excessive time with the employee, neglect other duties, neglect other employees, take too much work home, and build resentment toward that employee.

The very way you manage the employee probably suppresses his productivity. Sooner or later you will say, "See, I told you." You will have completed the self-fulfilling prophecy. Managers who expect more from their people get more. Teachers who expect higher grades get higher grades. Coaches who expect higher scores get higher scores. Why? Because their faith that their subordinates are capable of greater things is honest and sincere. They manage in the light of this faith, they transmit this faith, and the subordinates are motivated to higher achievement. Results? Greater productivity.

Determining Expectancy

Naturally, it would be sheer nonsense to think that employees could achieve anything, just because the manager felt they were capable of it. There is a matter of objectivity. Nor is an employee capable of achieving anything he wants merely by wanting to achieve it. Expectation must be realistic. But rare indeed is the manager whose expectations of subordinates are realistic. Reaching any degree of realism requires objective assessment of a subordinate's potential.

Making an objective assessment of an employee's potential will require a detailed study of *all* of the following factors regarding the employee:

Education, including courses studied
Hobbies, past and present (Many hobbyists bring special
    ingenuity and imagination to job situations.)
Work experience, including part-time jobs
Productivity in present job
Interest level in present job
Interest in other jobs
Plans for the future, goals, ambitions, and so on
Special skills and/or talents
Physical condition
Reaction to motivational efforts
Ability to take criticism
Reaction to challenges
Athletic interests (competitiveness)
Reading interests
Attitude toward management and company
Availability of in-job training
Motivational profile of the employee
Employee's self-image, as transmitted

Assessing these factors on an objective basis requires more than
a "seat of the pants" cursory consideration. Scanning over the employee's original application form will be of very little help. It will
probably provide no more than a list of sources to which you
should turn for some in-depth information.

The employee's transcripts from both high school and college
should be studied thoroughly to see which courses may lend themselves to growth in the job situation. The same is true of courses
taken, job assignments, and responsibilities in the military.

If employment tests were used, you should get a detailed analysis of the results from your director of personnel. Are aptitude
tests used? Personality profiles? Special interest tests of clerical,
mathematical, or verbal skills, listening comprehension, reading
comprehension, dexterity, mechanical aptitude, or other factors?
If such tests are not used, you may want to consider establishing
a battery of them for assessment purposes. In most cases such tests

are used after employment, not as a condition of employment, but they can provide a wealth of information relevant to what you may expect from your employees.

Much valuable information can be gained through face-to-face interviews with employees. Employees appreciate—and deserve—your interest in helping them grow within their jobs and in preparing them to assume greater responsibility.

Of great significance is the employee's own assessment of his capabilities as far as work is concerned. The employee may have special talents, skills, ideas, or interests of which you are totally unaware. Give the employee an opportunity to voice these things and you may be pleasantly surprised. It may also cause a substantial improvement in the employee's attitude toward the job. Employees want to be heard; let them.

Encourage your employees to discuss their jobs, ambitions, personal goals, capabilities, and interests. Encourage them to evaluate their potential objectively. Encourage them to grow in their jobs, to reach for greater things. Your encouragement may be the spark that brings about dramatic changes. But your encouragement is of little value unless you offer your wholehearted support in helping them reach those goals in the way of guidance, training, coaching, feedback, appraisal, and recognition for achievement. Job growth is not a "do-it-yourself " kit. It is a team activity. Remember your contractual arrangement with the employee, as discussed in Chapter 1.

Your expectations of an employee form an important part of the relationship between the two of you. The employee knows when you have a sincere faith in his ability and he will work harder to justify that faith.

During my management seminars, it doesn't take me very long to identify the managers who have high expectations of their employees and those whose expectations are pretty low. The managers who have low expectations utilize every coffee break to make a telephone call to their subordinates to see "how things are going." They *expect* problems. They *expect* to be needed. They *expect* their employees to ask for decisions.

What kind of message are these managers transmitting? They are saying, "You guys can't run the shop without me." Think of the negative motivational impact that has. If employees are that incompetent, there's only one person to blame—the manager. He makes them feel incompetent because he perceives them as incompetent and manages them as incompetents. His expectations are low and they respond accordingly.

Your employees will accept more responsibility readily when you display a sincere faith in their ability to handle it. They will strive for achievement for any manager who has faith in them—and shows it. Think of the many managers who are able to take a two-week vacation and never worry about their people. They never even call in to see if they are needed. Sure, they leave their itinerary with the employees so they can be contacted if necessary, but they leave it to their employees to initiate a telephone call. They have high expectations of their people and this relationship has a positive effect on staff output.

Furthermore, in this climate self-development becomes a way of life for the employees. This kind of manager not only wants his employees to grow, he knows they can grow—and they do grow. His expectations are based on faith, that complete, sincere confidence in their willingness, desire, and ability to achieve. The manager who has it is to be envied.

Evaluation of Supervisory Practices (ESP Rating)

1. Do I try objectively to assess my employees' potential, talent, and desire to grow in their jobs?
2. Do I openly display a sincere faith in their ability to achieve?
3. Do I encourage my employees to evaluate their potential objectively?
4. Do I really listen to my people?
5. Do I give my wholehearted support in helping my employees reach their personal and professional goals?

12 | Summary

It may appear that this book has presented an unrealistic "management by friendship" concept, one of being overly nice to everyone, turning them loose on blind faith, and making everyone love you. Nothing could be farther from the truth. What has been presented is a departure from the techniques we see used by so many managers today.

There is a desperate need for developing a healthy respect, a genuine respect, for our fellow employees. Managers must begin seeing all members of their staffs as intelligent, contributing, capable, and sensitive human beings, rather than as production expedients. The manager who has learned the true value of his employees is well on the way to developing a climate wherein high achievement is possible and will occur. This book has been designed to bring you, the manager, to that point.

But let's face reality. In the final analysis, *you* are totally responsible and accountable for the results of your work group. You are under an enormous amount of pressure to produce results. You are also the victim of many constraints—legal, corporate, ethical, time, budget, and policy, as well as self-imposed constraints. You must operate within the constraints and pressures of your job. These pressures will frequently detract from your efforts to develop healthy employee/supervisor relationships. But one responsibility must not be abdicated at the expense of the other.

There will be times when all your efforts to develop good employee relationships will be in vain. You will have to take stern disciplinary measures from time to time. But when the time comes, bite the bullet and do it. With some employees you may have to establish your position as a manager firmly at times, take an autocratic stand, and make some dictatorial demands. When the time comes for such action, take it!

There will be times when it becomes necessary to discharge an employee. If it is justified, have the fortitude to do it. But when you do, be certain that you can look back and honestly say you did everything possible to help the employee. You can't build an organization by firing people, and repair is usually more productive than replacement. It is far better to educate than to terminate.

It was stated earlier in this book that a company produces nothing—people produce everything. A business succeeds only because the people within that company succeed in their individual jobs. Professional teams win only because each individual on that team succeeds in his specific assignment.

By the same token, a business may fail if enough people in that company fail to meet their individual objectives and responsibilities. Granted, a few business failures can be attributed to economic conditions or other external factors over which the company has no control; however, this is true in only a small minority of cases. The vast majority of business failures are caused within that business.

Major contributing factors to failure include poor planning, poor product design, poor quality, poor marketing strategy, lack of customer concern, lack of financial control, and poor management practices. In every case, the fault can be laid right at the feet of management. The company failed because management allowed it to fail. On the other hand, a company succeeds because management causes it to succeed. That success comes when each manager causes his group to succeed. Group success, obviously, is the result of individual successes within that group.

Helping you to help your people succeed is what this book is about. If each of your people succeeds, you will succeed, and your group will have made a significant contribution toward the success of your company. You are vitally concerned about the overall success of your company, and you should be. But your primary responsibility is the success of the people to and for whom you are responsible, and your energy should be directed toward that end. Even if your entire company does not reach its objectives or full potential, *your* group will, if you make it happen.

I have tried throughout this book to present some of the management styles and practices that lead to group failure, so that you may avoid them. I have also presented many validated practices that lead to group success. The erroneous self-concept and the erroneous concept of others are two of the biggest causes of failure, because they foster management styles that are basically counterproductive. But there are other reasons managers fail. The emotionally insecure manager, for example, is either unwilling or afraid to manage by professional techniques, and this insecurity is transmitted right to his work group.

Unbalanced management, too, takes its toll. Managers tend to concentrate their efforts and attention on specific areas of interest and leave other areas neglected, to varying degrees. It is very easy to manage the "fun" areas and neglect the distasteful parts of the job, such as disciplinary situations, coaching, counseling, and training.

The successful manager balances his efforts and grasps his responsibilities from one end of the spectrum to the other. Therein lies the value of the management model presented in Chapter 1. It gives you a total and full perspective on your job as a manager. The model ties the job together in a logical format and logical sequence in the light of the interrelationships of the various functions.

It is important for any manager to apply his efforts to *all* the functions of the job. If a manager sees a unity among the segments of the job, he perceives the management task as one unified effort and tends to place an equal value on all segments. When this happens, group success is more likely.

If you were to think back through your own career, you could identify the managers you respected and those who fell short of your expectations. If you were to be objective in analyzing the qualities of those who held your respect, you would surely see that they placed equal emphasis on all aspects of the management job. Your comments about these managers would probably run in these veins:

"He listened to me."
"He respected me."
"He helped me."
"He was firm, but fair."
"He was consistent."
"He set a good example."
"He was interested in me."
"He understood people."
"You could depend on him."
"He made me stretch and grow."
"He was demanding, but realistic."
"You always knew where you stood with him."

The foregoing is not just theory or speculation. I can validate these comments. Scores of times, I have asked people in seminars to list the qualities or characteristics of their favorite managers. The responses were almost identical in every case. When I ask for the characteristics of the worst managers they have had, I invariably get reciprocal responses. It is important for a manager to consider the way in which people *want* to be managed, because management style has an enormous effect on employee attitudes, which, in turn, have a great effect on productivity.

The very best criteria we could follow would certainly be the management styles of successful managers. We should emulate those techniques that have positive and productive effects on people.

Professional managers understand people; they are sensitive to people; they listen to people; and they respond to people. As a result, their people reach high levels of achievement and follow a pattern of continued growth in the job. Employee turnover becomes almost nonexistent, except for those promoted into jobs of even greater responsibility.

Professional managers anticipate problems and manage in order to avoid them. They are not so enmeshed in the day-to-day activities that they fail to plan ahead. They recognize that most problems are internal and can be avoided. These managers avoid "management by crisis." They further realize that internal problems are caused—they are not accidental.

The following are some primary problems that professional managers anticipate, and the actions they take to prevent or avoid them.

High employee turnover
1. Plan ahead for manpower needs.
2. Match job/people specifications.
3. Select above-average people.
4. Train people thoroughly.
5. Provide continuous coaching and training.
6. Provide full-spectrum management of people.
7. Keep employees thoroughly informed at all times.

Lack of in-job growth
1. Provide challenging opportunities.
2. Recognize achievement.
3. Delegate to the maximum.
4. Provide training for growth.
5. Give constant encouragement.
6. Maintain high expectations.
7. Develop "stretching" goals.

Goals not being met
1. Have employee participation in goal setting.
2. Give necessary training and coaching.
3. Solicit employee suggestions.
4. Give plenty of feedback.
5. Provide positive reinforcement.
6. Keep all goals realistic.
7. Set a personal example.

Possible union organization
1. Provide good working conditions.
2. Provide adequate income.
3. Listen to employees, and respond to them.
4. Maintain an open-door policy.
5. Provide in-job growth.
6. Treat people as valuable human beings.

Manager's job overloaded
1. Select above-average people.
2. Train all employees religiously.
3. Delegate to the maximum.
4. Maintain high expectations.
5. Recognize achievement.
6. Allow maximum free rein.
7. Use participative management.
8. Display trust and faith in people.

Actions that can be taken to avoid anticipated problems all fall within the management model presented in Chapter 1. But problems can be avoided only through a practice of full-spectrum management. Not only will full-spectrum management make your job easier, it is what your employees deserve. It is all a part of your contractual arrangement. If you expect commitment, ability, and the drive to achieve, you must be willing to deputize, supervise, and energize.

Get to know your people well. A firm understanding of their

personalities is your key to motivating them. Understand that each of them is unique and must be managed as if he were the only person working for you. Understand that their values are different from each other's and different from yours. Accept them as individuals and manage them as such.

The intent of this book has not been to present a "buddy-buddy" style of dealing with people, but rather to present a style that leads to productivity and success. I do not believe in cow psychology—"Keep them contented and you will keep them productive." Quite the opposite is true. If you keep your people productive, you will keep them contented. Your people will be productive only when they want to be productive. Full-spectrum management develops that drive in people.

One of the basic characteristics of a productive work group is mutual respect between the manager and the employees. Respect cannot be unilateral in either direction. It can neither be demanded nor bought. It must be earned. You will earn the respect of your people when you meet your obligations under the contractual arrangement you have with them. Meeting those obligations may require you to change the way you have been managing people, at least to some degree. Perhaps it will require some changes in the way you view your people. These changes can be made with some disciplined effort on your part.

A lot of material—thoughts, ideas, concepts, and responsibilities—has been presented in this book. There are many things to be done and many things to be learned. But it is all part of being a manager of other people. When you accept a position of supervisor or manager, you accept everything that goes with it. Your employees are your responsibility. Their productivity is your responsibility. Their proficiency is your responsibility. Their growth is your responsibility. Why? Because it is you to whom they look for guidance, learning, encouragement, coaching, motivation, criticism, feedback, and recognition. These are the very justification for a manager's job.

It is your responsibility alone to see that the quantity and quality of output of your work group is as high as possible, meeting or exceeding your company's standards in every respect. Following the concepts presented in this book, coupled with a strong dedication to being a professional manager, will help you achieve that goal.

Obviously, you were looking for ways to improve your management effectiveness or you would never have read this far. One of the chief marks of a professional manager is the constant searching for a better way to manage others. I congratulate you on having that desire to grow and improve.

In the introduction to this book, I asked that you approach it with an open mind, that you read it all the way through and then draw your conclusions regarding management techniques that will help you grow. I hope you have found suggestions that will do just that.

As you conclude this summary chapter, I suggest that you go back through the ESP rating lists at the ends of the chapters and see whether you have found some changes in both technique and thinking. If so, you have learned and grown. As a result, your work group will also learn and grow—and therein lies the real payoff.

You are serving two worlds with entirely different values: management and employees. You have an equal responsibility to each. Maintain a fair balance of loyalty to each at all times. You are responsible to your company and its objectives. But you are also responsible to your employees. All deserve every professional effort you can muster. When both your company and your employees are getting your best effort and know they are getting it, you will truly be a professional manager, and both your company and employees will be aware of it. It is my sincere hope that I have, in some way, helped you reach that point. I have tried to bring you the best of the best. The rest is up to you.

Index

173

unilateral contract with employees, 21
union organization, as problem of
management, 170

value of deviation, as factor in consequences, 146

verification, of application data,
48–49

"will do" factors, in motivation,
121
work experience, as hiring standard, 43